HAIRAPY

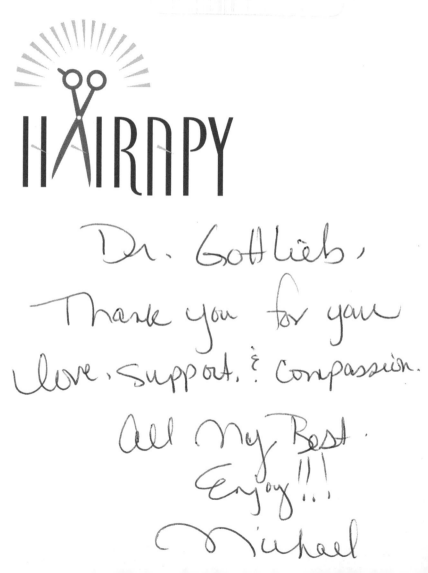

Dr. Gottlieb,

Thank you for your love, support, & compassion.

All My Best.

Enjoy!!!

Michael

HAIRAPY
DEEPER THAN THE ROOTS
by MICHAEL BLOMSTERBERG

MLR Publishing
Los Angeles, California

Hairapy: Deeper than the Roots by Michael Blomsterberg

Published by MLR Publishing
8033 Sunset Blvd. #817
Los Angeles, CA 90046-2401

Cover design by Rapture Studio
www.rapturestudio.com

Interior design by Pneuma Books, LLC.
For more info, visit www.pneumabooks.com

Publisher's Cataloging-In-Publication Data
(*Prepared by The Donohue Group, Inc.*)

Blomsterberg, Michael.
   Hairapy : deeper than the roots / by Michael Blomsterberg.

   p. ; cm.

   ISBN: 0-9777852-1-1

1. Personal coaching. 2. Self-help techniques. 3. Self-realization.
4. Conduct of life. I. Title.

BF637.P36 B55 2006
158/.1   2006922560

11 10 09 08 07 06   6 5 4 3 2 1

I dedicate this book to each and every one of you looking for peace, love, acceptance, and fulfillment. May you find it within. Celebrate you, for you are the gift.

Contents

PREFACE

I wrote this book because I believe in people. I believe that our truth lies within each and every one of us and that by allowing ourselves the permission to journey inward, limitless possibilities await us.

I see everything as an opportunity—an opportunity to deepen our capacity of love, faith, compassion, understanding, acceptance and gratitude.

I have taken complete responsibility for my life and for all of my life's experiences. This liberty has brought me tremendous freedom, the power of choice, and infinite mobility. It's a blessing to feel safe in the world in which I live. I invite you to consider your accountability in the totality of your life.

Many of us define ourselves by our accomplishments, our results, our physicality, our outcomes. We (unconsciously) run as fast as we can. We run from feelings that threaten to overwhelm us at our core. Stillness seems almost unfathomable. Will anything ever be *enough*?

In today's world of *doing*, I find *being* to be under-valued. Yes, I am proud of my accomplishments, but I am more fulfilled by who I am.

We are all perfect, beautiful, and whole exactly as we are. What will it feel like to receive that? Trust. You are magnificent.

chapter 1
WELCOME to the SALON

I have been fortunate in my career as a hairapist to have loyal clients. I have been scheduled six months in advance for years and rarely had to advertise. While the focus of my salon has shifted from hair to personal coaching, it continues to be the fun, relaxing place it has always been and my practice of hairapy remains the same. I devote all my personal resources to simply being with my clients, accepting them for who they are, loving them as they are, and helping them make the very subtle, simple changes that can take their lives from the automatic to the authentic.

An automatic life is one many of us understand. When we compare ourselves to others in order to evaluate our own worth, when we value external achievement more than internal well-being, we are living from an automatic place. I know many people who are successful, powerful, wealthy, and wildly unhappy — because their lives are on automatic pilot and have been for a long time.

Automatic pilot means we are seeking what we have been taught to seek: love, approval, money, power, and beauty. Like so many other human doings, we are racing to get the right clothes and the right products and striving to think the right thoughts and feel the right feelings. In general, we are occupied with fulfilling the conscious and unconscious demands of the world.

An authentic life is unique for everyone. This fact has made the writing of this book, quite frankly, an interesting challenge. On the one hand, I know that many of you want to change your lives, lose weight, find relationships, make more money, and in general feel better. I applaud that, and there are programs and professionals devoted to helping you organize, prioritize, and act in ways designed to help you achieve those results. But my approach requires an important distinction. I don't teach you how to get results or make changes directly. My work is not about DOING. I teach you how to welcome new experiences, new beliefs, new opportunities, and new people into your life. My work is about BEING. It's about each of us giving ourselves permission to be the totality of who we are with no apologies, reservations, or limits.

I have seen stunning and profound transformations using this approach. My own was the first. I have survived physical and psychological abuse, bulimarexia, bankruptcy, drug and alcohol addiction, and testicular cancer. Slowly but surely I appreciated these challenges, learned the lessons they brought to my life, and harnessed my new understanding to contribute to the lives of others. I have had only good fortune.

You are not normal. You are special. Your opportunities to contribute to this world are unlike any other. When you can learn to see yourself as the magnificent being you are, all the changes you desire will not only be possible, they will already be manifesting. Have faith, and join me to create the world behind your eyes. That is where the true gold lies.

Enjoy!

chapter 2
NOTICE YOURSELF

When most of us look in the mirror, we are not noticing ourselves. We're judging ourselves. Many of us have self-concepts sourced in judgment and self-esteem to match. We feel as though we are never enough. However, each of us, at this very moment, is enough. We each have the capacity right now to begin creating the life we desire. The question is then, why do we still feel as though we are never enough?

The answer is simple — we need to get to know ourselves better.

Let me make a suggestion: as experienced as you may be, as much as you know about the world and about yourself, why not allow for the possibility that there are areas of your conscious and unconscious self that you don't know very well? Can you engage in a process of discovery with yourself?

Perhaps the most important tool for your toolbox is being able to observe yourself in the moment in a non-judgmental way. It is a skill you will practice over and over as you read this book, and one you can use throughout the course of your life. It is the key that unlocks the door to living your dream-come-true life: one of meaning, fulfillment, enjoyment, health, love, and peace.

You, at this moment, are different than at any other moment in your entire life. You have memories of a past that no longer exists. You have expectations of a future that also does not exist. The only thing that exists is the present moment. There is no future you. There is no past you. There is only you right now.

This is so important. Part of the reason it can be challenging for many of us to notice ourselves is because we're used to being who we think we are. That consistency makes us feel safe. We know what to expect from ourselves. Others know how to behave toward us. It's funny — even though we want to change, there is a part of us that wants to keep everything exactly the same.

Therefore, in noticing ourselves, we must allow for the possibility that we will notice something new.

This is why making neutral, non-judgmental observations is so important — because novelty disappears in a context of judgment.

At any moment, you have permission to take a tiny step back and ask yourself one or more questions to help you notice yourself in that moment:

- What am I feeling right now?
- What am I thinking right now?
- What bodily sensations am I experiencing right now?
- How am I behaving right now?
- What is most important to me right now?
- What do I want out of this moment?

This is the beginning of the journey available to all of us. Noticing ourselves, we track down the sources of our discontent and also of our joy. We discover nuggets of valuable information, energy, and personal resources hidden deep within. As we practice observing ourselves without judgment, accepting any feeling or thought we have without reservation, we begin to know ourselves better.

To notice yourself is to know yourself, and as the song says, to know you is to love you. You may not feel lovable, but I promise you, there are parts of you that are crying out for attention: repressed parts, secret parts, parts that fill out the rest of the authentic you, and those parts are desperate to be seen, heard, and acknowledged. Noticing yourself is an act of self-love and it's time to start right now, in this moment.

So take a deep breath. Notice your body, energy, thoughts and feelings. You may see that you're in pain, or locked up in judgment, and that's okay — notice that. You may see yourself jubilant, ecstatic, satisfied, peaceful — simply notice. The beauty of noticing yourself is that you can do it anytime, anywhere, and in any emotional state. You can do it while exercising. You can do it in the middle of an argument. You can do it when you first get up in the morning or when you're driving and a song lyric triggers something inside you.

The results of noticing yourself are profound. Because you are willing to notice anything, anything at all, without limits, you create limitless possibilities for who you are and who you might become. This is an act of deep self-respect essential to creating the life for yourself that you truly desire.

chapter 3
SCALES and What to Do with Them

Forget scales. Screw measuring yourself and comparing yourself to others. We have so many ways to inappropriately evaluate ourselves: weight, height, bank account, attractiveness, intelligence. Have you ever truly benefited or gained new and valuable information from comparing yourself to other people?

Suppose I compare my lot to that of a starving child in Africa. I live in the midst of abundance while he's dying from malnutrition and living on a dollar a day, if that. The comparison doesn't make my financial challenges disappear. It doesn't make an extra slice of Chicago-style deep-dish any easier to resist. Or how about when I compare myself to the guys on the cover of *Men's Health*? That's a sure recipe for inner peace.

Do you keep a scale in your bathroom? Well, unless

you're an Olympic wrestler, you might as well get a little bench and throw a noose around a ceiling beam and jump — it will be far less painful in the long-term. Tying your self-esteem to a number and evaluating yourself every day? Sure, I've done it, many of us have, but does it sound sane? Measuring self-worth with a number? A *number*? It's insanity, pure insanity.

Measure yourself against people you perceive to be better off and you just inflame your jealousy. Measure yourself against people you perceive to be worse off and you invalidate your turmoil. Measure yourself against you as you were three years ago, five years ago, or in college, and that's just nuts! You're not the same person. The past is gone! Vive la present! Comparing you to yourself in days gone by is mental masturbation that puts limits on who you can be now.

We compare ourselves to other people, because our eyes face out. So that's where we look. We look outside of who we are in the moment, we compare ourselves to this or that, we get jealous, we measure and re-measure, and it doesn't work because our true identity lies inside, not outside. We can only love, accept, and stand in our own uniqueness. There's no comparison to make.

chapter 4
Your WORLD
Is Your MIRROR

When you look into the mirror, what do you see? You might notice your posture, your musculature, your physical size and shape. You might notice the choices you've made about how to wear your hair, the products you use for your skin, the clothes you choose and how they fit. Your physical being tells a story of who you are.

The same is true of your home, be it grand or ever so humble. Where do you keep your stuff? Do you have stacks and piles? Do you organize? Is your home clean, dirty, messy, neat? What's in your fridge? Where is the energy flowing? Where is the energy blocked? Look around your space — what clues do you see about who lives there? Any good detective knows that a person's space discloses a version of who they are.

Notice your friends, your social world. When you see your friends, you see yourself. You project your desires onto them, they project their desires onto you. You like things in them that you like about yourself, and you find certain things irritating about them that you find objectionable in yourself. They do the same thing. We magnetize people to us who are teachers and students, people to whom we have something to give and from whom we have something to receive. Our personalities are like radio stations broadcasting our unique music. Consciously and unconsciously everyone around us is picking up the signal. Friends are those who tune in and listen. Therefore, your social world reveals a lot about who you are.

The challenge is to realize that who we are exists at many different levels and extends beyond our conscious minds. In other words, you and I each manifest our reality at every moment. We have options when it comes to how we eat and exercise and sit and sleep and dress and spend money. We decide where to live and how often to clean up and where our various objects should be placed. We choose our friends and our jobs. Each of us is our own world, and we create it to help us learn. This is why so much of what we manifest is difficult, troubling, and painful. It's because, sometimes, that's the only way we will pay attention, listen, and learn.

To enjoy your reality more, accept it. Have some compassion for yourself. Have some mercy on yourself. Look at your world and, gently, tell the truth about what you see so that you can begin to welcome the changes you want into your life.

How do we do this? We take ownership of what we see in the mirror.

Your social world is a mirror:

- Who are your friends? What do you like or dislike about them?
- Who are your family members? What is your family role?
- What social situations are especially comfortable or uncomfortable?

Your home is a mirror:

- How does the energy (chi) flow through your home?
- In which areas are you most comfortable?

- Where is the clutter? Where is the light?

Your body is a mirror:

- How is your health?
- How do you feel right now?
- What are you wearing?

Your mind is a mirror:

- What thoughts pass through your brain all the time?
- What themes occur frequently in your dreams?
- What is important to you? In your world, what matters?

I know you're someone who prides yourself on being honest, so get honest and call a spade a spade. It's not an excuse to be brutal; simply be kind and be honest. There's no need to whip yourself. Instead, welcome yourself. Observe your world with gentle eyes and see what's around. It's you, and moreover, you asked for it. Now — what are you going to learn from what you see?

chapter 5
The HOLIDAYS?
The HELLIDAYS?

Ah, the holidays. A time of joy, love, and the highest suicide rate of the year! Good food, family, friends, and the kind of fighting and emotional turbulence that makes you want to snort uncrushed Dexedrine. Fun!

Let's take a flying leap and assume, just for fun, that time with your family, especially over the holidays, *might* be stressful. After all, our relatives are people who have played a significant role in the development of our personality. These are people who can push our psychological hot-buttons with an inadvertent remark, if not with an outright attack. These are the people who helped design and install those buttons. Consciously or unconsciously, these are also the people who enjoy pressing them the most.

Family holiday events can be crises waiting to happen — which is a good thing. The Chinese character or word for *crisis* also means "opportunity," and this is how you turn the hellidays into the holidays. You use the experience for your own emotional, psychological, and spiritual growth.

Here's an example. One thing that relatives often do (unconsciously) is treat you like someone you used to be. Some family members might always remember you as an adorable kid who screamed when people took pictures of him, some might remember the rebellious teenager with a D. U. I., some never even really knew you at all and have no one to remember. You know what I'm talking about — it's that feeling where you sigh to yourself, "It's like I never left home."

That's not a fun feeling. You deserve love and support unconditionally, right? You deserve to be seen and appreciated for who you truly are, right? And now these people, who are supposed to love you, don't seem to get who you really are! How can they love you when they don't even see you?

This is a crisis, yes. But it is also an opportunity. It's a chance for you to notice the difference in how they treat you and how you would like to be treated. It's a chance to see your relatives as people — not as mother, father, sister, but as Bonnie, Anthony, Rebecca. It's a chance to take a stand as the person you are, not the person you were (or the person they thought you were), and to change how you participate in your family dynamics.

If you're not ready to take this opportunity, consider this: there is no law that says that you must spend holiday time with your biological relatives. You have permission to go wherever you want or nowhere at all. If you feel like you must go, that there's no escaping your duty to go, that's okay, too. You have permission to feel obligated. So long as you recognize the truth, which is that you can go where you want — even if you want to act out of obligation.

You also have permission to go spend time with your relatives as yourself — and not who you perceive they would like you to be. If you're a recent grad, bitter about the post-college job market, there's no need to be perfect daughter Mary Sunshine for the holidays. Perhaps you're in a new relationship with someone you perceive no one will like and you plan on biting your tongue every time you're asked if you're dating. Hey, no matter what, be yourself. Be argumentative. Be non-confrontational. Be a wallflower. Keep your balance, or don't. There's nothing wrong with getting upset — there's so much to learn if you can be conscious and aware as well.

Because we can anticipate some bumps in our holiday travel plans, it makes sense to pack a few extras. Bring your ability to notice yourself. Bring boundaries, so you know precisely where you're prepared to take a stand. Bring a safety net, like a friend you can call late at night or a journal for some cathartic writing or a talisman of magical protection, like a rock from the Pacific Ocean, or a Snickers bar. Bring whatever thoughts, feelings, and objects best serve and protect you.

I believe that feeling loved is so important. Loving and being loved is euphoric and satisfying. It's like eating a great meal when you're hungry or falling asleep after a hard day's work or being held when you're crying and afraid. Feeling loved is more important than being with people who are supposed to love you. For that reason my family includes close friends and certain clients and mentors as well as many of my biological relatives.

The people I keep close to me — my family — see me, love me, and appreciate me for who I am. Who have you chosen to be a part of your family?

chapter 6
ANCIENT TRAUMA
or Buried Treasure?

The biggest lie that people live is that they're going to live forever. Death is a fact and with awareness of death comes enrichment of life. This is why people who have accidents that result in near-death experiences, or who survive terminal diseases, or who are simply nearing the end of their days often live gracefully and powerfully. The proximity of death throws the rest of their lives into sharp focus, allowing them to feel love for others, connection to the world, and gratitude for small things.

To your ego, however, personality transformation isn't much different from physical death. We avoid situations and people that might provoke change, and at the same time we inexorably seek the very experiences that will transform us. Similarly, we avoid situations where we might physically die even though we are moving toward that end. The point here is this: you don't need a near-death experience or a terminal disease to have awareness of your death and appreciation for your life. You do have to experience change, however, and one of the great fuels for change is illness — where the transformation of the personality and the deterioration of the body intertwine like a caduceus.

This is tricky because illness doesn't deserve to be demonized, but the truth is that none of us want to be sick. It's not just the discomfort or pain, it's the total vulnerability, the asking for help, the lack of control — not to mention lost time at work. However, since getting sick is an inevitable part of life, let's give ourselves permission to benefit from the experience.

When you're sick, you can't help but be sick. So in that sense, you're already on the road to transformative healing. You also can't help but feel how you feel. However, fear can make it hard to see what's going on, namely that you're being given an opportunity for rest, healing, and transformation. This is what I mean when I say that illness is a gift. When you appreciate the opportunity, the vast amount of energy you will expend to get better will be put to the best use.

Here's an example. Lance Armstrong has won the Tour de France, the most challenging endurance race in the world, an unprecedented seven times. He has also survived testicular cancer. What's the relationship between these two facts? If you listen to the way the media covers Armstrong, they say things like, "He's such a gifted athlete, such a talented competitor, that he's able to win despite his cancer."

But if you read his book, *It's Not About the Bike*, I think you'll come to a different conclusion: he wins (in part) *because* of his cancer. Cancer helped Lance sharpen his priorities as well as feel tremendous gratitude and appreciation for his family, his body, and his ability to compete in an event like the Tour de France. Lance, with tremendous courage, developed his life and his career into the life he'd always wanted. Cancer was a major catalyst of this transformation.

When you get sick to any degree, whether it's a mild sickness like the flu or a serious, life-threatening illness, one of the first things that happens is a shifting of priorities. The sicker you are, the faster things become clear. Money and material concerns fade into the background. Love, joy, intimacy and pleasure take precedence. Your heart opens; you often relish vulnerability and the unknown. Others have the privilege to take care of you, and you get to give them that gift.

Sonia Johnson said, "What we resist, persists." What we deny, remains. It's such wonderful common sense. We experience trauma and we deny it (or we deny how much it affects us). This denial is an energetic force that remains inside us, waiting for a moment when it can re-emerge. We re-create the original trauma again and again so those emotions can resurface. If we continue to deny them, they morph into other emotions and resistances. For example, if you can't handle your anger, it can manifest as depression. If you can't handle your depression, you might start eating compulsively. Soon, what began as a trauma in childhood results in obesity in adulthood. It's not about what we're eating, it's what's eating us.

Another way of saying this is, your emotional and spiritual and social life absolutely positively impacts your health. When your health is threatened, it's almost always an opportunity to correct imbalances in the present and heal wounds from the past (the ancient trauma) and to transform them into energy, health, gratitude, and love (the buried treasure).

Faith is the accelerator, fear is the brake. We fear change, we fear the unknown, and we fear being out of control of our lives, even when we're sick. Thus, we resist what's happening in the present moment. We don't want to be sick and so we judge sickness as bad. This fear, this judgment, slows the process down. See illness as a gift and realize that everything is happening just as it's supposed to, even if you don't understand. Allow your priorities and relationships to deepen and evolve. Use the opportunity to heal the ancient wounds that are the foundation of your illness and harness new health and energy for the moments to come.

chapter 7
YOU Are a HERO

In a movie, the hero desires a particular goal beyond all else and confronts an obstacle that's very much in the way. To achieve her goal, a movie hero takes risks, like diving into frozen rivers and rushing into burning buildings. Although these actions are extreme, they are appropriate metaphors for our own lives.

You see, the journey of the movie hero is an externalized (and stylized) version of the path we all walk internally. We are each heroic. We are each living a story. At a given moment, there is something we want beyond all else, and at that same moment, there is some enormous obstacle that's in our way. To achieve our goals, we must risk. With compassion, with patience, and with faith, we must risk rejection, looking stupid, being abandoned, having a secret exposed, letting go of a crutch or pacifier.

Consider how we can be the greatest impediment to ourselves. For many of us, our goal is to live a life of freedom and enjoyment and purpose. What stops us? Frequently, it's ourselves, our baggage, our unconscious. So what do we do? We work with books like this, we go to therapy, we seek out the burning buildings within and rush inside to save ourselves.

Think of yourself as a character in a movie and consider these questions. What is most important to your character? What are his or her goals? What really gets your character excited? What's in the way?

Answering questions like these is an ongoing process. Our lives are stories piled on top of each other, sequences of short films, novels, movies, TV episodes. We are heroes in multiple stories.

The key is to see yourself for who you are and to be accountable. After all, you create your world. You've set up problems for yourself to solve, you're in relationships with people who are teachers and allies, you've already chosen a story and passed out scripts. Everyone is playing a part and you've got the starring role.

Now what happens? What happens is that one day, you become hip to yourself. You see how you've set things up. You see who's playing what part. You see who you are and you take accountability for yourself and your world.

This can be delicious. When you leap into the unknown, you may discover that you are not the person you thought you were — but you may also discover the person you always knew you could be.

chapter 8
UNIVERSAL CHEMISTRY

Every living and non-living being, every idea, every molecule, is connected to everything else. We may think of ourselves as unique individuals, and we are, but we are also an inextricable part of the magnificent whole.

Imagine that you're on a date in a new restaurant. Look around. See the restaurant. See your date. Now, realize this: you are connected to the entire world.

Consider the restaurant itself. It was built, renovated, decorated. That means architects, construction workers, zoning officials at city hall, inspectors, furniture salesmen, designers. Every object in the restaurant needed to be manufactured — every china plate, every knife and fork, every champagne glass, every tablecloth — everything. That means scientists and idea people, technology people, people who build and maintain the factories, people who transport the objects across the country. Your food is picked, caught, cleaned, frozen, shipped, prepared — all using countless individuals, machines, and technologies. Fundamentally, the price and availability of food is directly related to world commodities markets, global weather patterns, and the state of the planet in general. Your meal is sourced, in no small part, by the history of world civilization to this point.

But let's get back to the date. Suppose there's great chemistry. What does chemistry mean? The conversation flows, there's lots of laughter, knowing looks, flirting. It also means transformation. That's what chemistry is — two substances react and both are changed in the process. The presence of your being changes the other person, and the presence of their being changes you. Each of you leaves an energetic footprint in the other person's world.

The choices you make in your life, down to the smallest detail, reverberate through everyone with whom you come into contact and beyond. Everyone's a role model for everyone else. So, if you're on a first date and having great chemistry, you're also in a chemical reaction with the waiter, the chef, the other patrons, and the restaurant as a whole. In fact, you're in a chemical reaction with the whole universe *at every moment*. This is your legacy: the energetic footprint you leave wherever you go.

Gandhi said, "Be the change you wish to see in the world." This is an especially profound statement because of its underlying assumption — that by changing oneself, it is possible to change the world. After all, many of us have issues with the government, with world politics, with what's on TV, and more. Now we have an avenue to make positive changes. We adapt internally. We understand the interconnectedness of all things. By making adjustments to ourselves, in the long run, we are being the change we wish to see in the world.

How do you live your life? What do you value? What beliefs do you cherish? For example, how do you feel about change? If you have accepted and embraced change in your own life, then an environment of possibility surrounds you. People in your space can contemplate adventures, explore their dreams, and simply be themselves.

Perhaps you feel unhappy with who you are and you're inclined to believe there's nothing to be done about it. Perhaps you think the world's inevitably going to hell in a handbasket. Now the environment around you is one of impossibility, judgment, and suffocation. People around you may doubt themselves, feel stifled, or even criticized without you having to say a word.

However, if you source yourself in possibility, compassion, and acceptance, you are giving a gift to others and the world around you. Faith-based thoughts like appreciation, gratitude, delight, and pleasure catalyze your interaction with the world. Fear-based thoughts like worry, doubt, resentment, and stress limit your interaction with the world. Thus, if you feed on impossibility, guilt, anger, denial, and suffering, you will feel increasingly isolated.

Look around yourself right now. Can you see the interconnectedness of all things? What kinds of thoughts and beliefs source you? What kind of chemistry do you experience with the universe?

chapter 9
IDENTIFY What You WANT

Sometimes, what we think we want isn't what we really want. All of us, at some point, have realized a major goal — perhaps getting married, having a baby, getting a great job, selling a script, winning an Oscar — the experience of triumph is great for a day or two, maybe a week … and then it's gone.

Achieving a goal can feel disappointing because you're done with the chase, the pursuit, the journey. However, many of us don't enjoy the journey, and the achieved goal often does not sustain us. That's a double-whammy and an invitation to reconsider our goals. Have you chosen your goals? Are your achievements your own?

To really understand this, we need to go back to childhood. It is a fact that many if not most parents unconsciously use their children to meet their own emotional needs. Obvious examples include many young professional athletes — how many tennis players and quarterbacks have parents who want their children to have the fame and fortune that they never had themselves? What about child actors and pageant kids? How about everyone who just "knows" at an early age that they want to be a doctor or a lawyer? Can you imagine how far this dynamic extends beyond the profession your parents would have you choose? Can you imagine how far children will go to please their parents?

Why do many parents take their children from activity to activity? Is it because the kids have requested non-stop days of instruction? Maybe. My guess is that parents are using their children to keep themselves busy, distracting themselves much in the same way they'd watch TV or shop all day long.

Furthermore, many parents want to be validated. They want to know that they are good parents — and they prove it to themselves by their child's performance. When you're three or five or eleven or sixteen and your parents are determining their worth and self-esteem from your games and recitals and grades, the fun of being a kid quickly turns into hard work.

Let's pause here for a sec. I'm not saying that activities are bad for children or that parents shouldn't be invested in their child's performance. I'm simply pointing out how and where these activities can go awry.

Let's look at a mild example, a typical moment in a typical childhood. The parent is driving the child home from a lesson.

Parent: "Did you have a good time?"

Child: "Uh-huh."

Parent: "Great! Tell me all about it."

This moment is the kind of moment most of us spend our lives trying to recover from. The reason is because the child wants to please the parent. The child knows that the lesson is important to the parent — that he or she is supposed to enjoy the hour of camp or piano or soccer or whatever — and so when the child is asked a question, he's probably not going to answer with his or her truth. The parent doesn't want to hear the truth. The parent wants to hear what she wants to hear, namely that she was right to pay for the lesson and her child loves it — which means she's a good parent.

Parent: "Did you have a good time?"

Child: "Umm... not really."

Parent: "Oh. Why not? What's wrong this time?"

A kid doesn't want to have this conversation. It's intimidating. The reason is because the parent, having a vested interest in the child continuing lessons, is now asking the child to justify his feelings with evidence. This is an adult conversation and it is scary for two reasons: first, the child doesn't know how to participate in this kind of conversation; second, and more importantly, it shows that the child's well-being isn't the parent's top priority.

This example is pretty mild and may not speak to you directly, so let me summarize in another way: it is the nature of children to want to please their parents. However, parents are often still people who have not become adults. They may be in their thirties or forties or fifties with children of their own, but they are still trying to please *their* parents, so they enlist their children to help them in their own unconscious mission. This dynamic is a part of so many parent-child interactions.

Identifying what we want is a process that takes place on both the spiritual and material levels. The spiritual level has to do with our life's purpose. Let the expectations of friends and relatives and the concerns of the world drift away. What do *you* want? Is the journey of your life one that speaks to your heart? What do you value? What's important to you? What do you really enjoy?

The material level is where life is lived day-to-day. For example, you might find yourself in a disagreement with your partner. Take a moment and ask yourself a few questions. What do I want? What do I really want out of this conversation? Is it to be right? Is it to understand my partner? Is it to get them to understand me? Or, suppose you are caught in traffic and getting upset. What do you want? Perhaps it's to get home as quickly as possible, so you might take an alternate route. Perhaps it's simply to avoid being upset, and so you put on some music, or even stop to use the bathroom or get a snack. Knowing what you want is the first step toward acting on your own behalf and makes receiving what you want possible.

Goals are often given to us — not chosen by us. Without a process to clarify our own specific goals and intentions, we may fall back on a mixture of what our parents gave us long ago and the cultural goals that are the norm, like being rich, thin, powerful, successful, attractive, correct, and so forth. If you choose to pause for a moment, look around, and determine what you want out of a given situation, your instincts and your mind and your heart and your spirit can start to work together for a common purpose. If you cannot journey inward to discover your true nature, you will be forever living your life to please others.

chapter 10
You Have to DIE to DIET

Someone once said, "It's not what you're eating, it's what's eating you." This is an interesting aphorism. On the one hand, it helps us focus on our diet as an internal journey. It helps us pay attention to the uncomfortable feelings inside of us that we soothe with food. On the other hand, it sets us up in an adversarial relationship with our feelings — after all, they're "eating" us.

The truth is, our feelings aren't eating us. They are parts of us, and we can appreciate them. Uncomfortable feelings — even powerful ones like depression, despair, guilt, jealousy, shame, anger, grief, and sadness — are the bearers of important and life-changing lessons. Being your authentic self means experiencing these feelings and learning these lessons.

However, many of us have created identities rooted in denial. Consider why we embark on a new diet. We often do it for superficial reasons. We diet to fit into a new pair of jeans, to lose weight, look better, to snag Mr. Right. We start a diet and weigh ourselves more often, check ourselves in the mirror constantly. So many of us start diets because we do not accept ourselves. We want to change how we look because we think that will change who we are.

Let's notice this. It's kind of funny that many of us start diets to change who we are, when a diet is really a journey of self-acceptance. We must see the truth of our eating habits and our internal worlds. We must understand and accept that how we feed our body is a metaphor for how we feed our spirit. In short, achieving the goal of changing ourselves requires accepting ourselves, and this opposition can make dieting a frustrating endeavor.

I know more than a little about this. Let's just say that I never really grew fond of my newfound back fat. You name it, I've tried it: Jenny Craig, Tony Robbins, Richard Simmons, and Susan Powter. Oh, and liposuction around my waist — which by the way is great (if you happen to change your eating habits). I was always looking outside of myself for what needed to be an internal exploration.

It wasn't until I was willing to roll up my sleeves and go inward that this roller coaster ceased to exist. Welcoming all of my feelings and accepting that all colors are valid truly saved my life.

Acceptance is like a fire. It has the potential to burn away anything that's not pure and true, and this is what I mean when I say that you have to die to diet. You have to be willing to let your current incarnation die off and allow a more authentic you to emerge. You have to be willing to let this happen slowly and in bursts over a great deal of time. It's one of the great journeys of life and it requires patience, love, compassion, and understanding.

Rather than thinking about changing what we eat in order to change our lives, consider that by accepting what we eat, we can begin to accept life. If we do that, change occurs without us doing any "changing." You might start by simply noticing what you eat. See it. Feel how you feel before eating, during, and afterwards. Be the person you are, the person with those feelings, those eating habits, those food choices. Your process of adaptation and change has begun.

Have you ever seen a TV personality tell a woman that in order to lose weight she must fix her marriage? This is a brute force approach and it sounds pretty tough. To lose thirty pounds, this woman's going to have to up-end her life, shake up her marriage, potentially affect her children, and risk altering her performance at work.

Now, there are good aspects to this approach. It identifies issues at a deeper level and it honors the woman's stated goal — that of losing weight. Let's follow this pathway out to the logical conclusion: to change herself, she must change her marriage. To change her marriage, she must face her own internal issues and challenges and change herself deep inside. To change deep inside, she must begin to accept herself… and now we're back to where we started. Change is created through acceptance, through consciousness.

My suggestion to you is to start this process where you are going to finish it anyway — with acceptance. Start with compassion toward yourself. Start gently. It's good to understand that diet is a massive and magnificent undertaking. It's good to know that as you learn more, as you make adjustments in one area of your life, you will likely need to make adjustments in other areas as well. Begin this process and continue this process from a foundation of self-care, self-acceptance, and self-love.

Change is not a verb in this context. We do not

change ourselves. We experience change. It's created by acceptance, by seeing yourself, feeling your feelings, and being who you are.

This idea is a really tough one to understand at a deep level because of how our culture is defined by doing. We put causes into motion, we see effects. We push a button and something happens. We use *change* as a verb all the time. We make adjustments at work and in communication with a partner; we make choices about what goes into our mouths at lunchtime; we are changing and making changes constantly. The outcome of this is that we believe that we are in control of our world. We believe that we have the capacity to make changes to anything.

Now, in a sense, we do, but there is an important difference between welcoming change and forcing change. Forcing is what most of us mean when we say that we're "making changes." This is why so many diets don't work. We only know how to use willpower — to discipline and force ourselves to make changes.

This, quite simply, is not effective in the long term. Willpower is the match that lights the fire, not the wood that burns. There's no staying power in forcing yourself. Furthermore, using willpower, that special reserve of psychological energy reserved for emergencies, depletes us — making us vulnerable to trading addictions. Drop the thirty pounds, but pick up smoking. Quit smoking, but start shopping until your credit cards are maxed out. Repair your financial situation and dive into codependent relationships. In other words, the more serious you are about losing weight, the more committed you are to changing your life, the more you must stop forcing yourself. Instead, see yourself, be yourself, feel everything, and gently allow yourself to change.

chapter 11
The CULTURE of THIN

There's a big difference between being an American and being a consumer. The basis of the American culture is freedom and individuality. These are adult values. Being a consumer, in a way, is like being a child. You're told where to go and you go. You're told what to do and you do it. Only in this case, mommy's not giving the orders. It's culture. It's advertising, marketing, and selling.

One of the factors rarely taken into account when it comes to losing weight and living a healthier lifestyle goes beyond what you're putting into your mouth — it's what you're putting into your brain. In order to reclaim our physical, mental, and emotional health, we must learn to make common sense choices without being persuaded by the people trying to sell to us.

For example, do you read labels? It's the only way to

know exactly what you're eating. Do you trust food companies to tell you the truth about how much salt and fat and sugar are in your food? Do you trust them to list all the chemicals they use in processing and preserving your food?

Be alert. Labels have been around for a long time, but the laws that require food companies to really tell us what's in the food they're selling were passed in the last decade.[1] You might already know that many food companies spend more on the packaging of the food than the food itself — what does that tell you about their priorities? Who do you think makes more money — the guy who grows the food, the guy who works in the factory that processes the food, or the guy who designs the package to entice you to buy the food? How about the guy who runs the focus group to ask three groups of twelve people which packaging they prefer?

Many of us, when we look at a lifestyle-magazine cover, feel inadequate. We're supposed to. You see, the standard for beauty has become superhuman, artificial, impossible to achieve — but the purpose of the magazine is, ostensibly, to help us achieve this impossible vision. How? By educating, entertaining, and ... selling us stuff.

---

[1] American Technology Preeminence Act of 1991

Nutrition Labeling and Education Act of 1990 (NLEA)

That's why right after the picture of a supermodel or a collection of very beautiful people, there's a bottle of alcohol or a fashion ad or a fancy watch or a hamburger. The idea is to stimulate you to feel crappy, and then as soon as possible, stimulate you to feel good. Voila! You feel the need to buy. Versions of this technique are everywhere. Every ad is saying, "Look who you're not," and, "Look at what you don't have." Then, once they've established our unworthiness, the ads say, "All your problems solved — just consume this."

Gaining and losing weight is one of the economic machines that make our culture work. For example, consider all of the products and services designed to help you lose weight: how many of them are sourced in the desire to improve your health, and how many are simply trying to get your money? Consider most of the food industry and the restaurant business: how many of these companies and restaurants emphasize your health? How many function like heroin dealers — where your addiction is their repeat business?

Now consider the advertising techniques used by both sides. The weight-loss people remind you of how crappy you feel before they offer you their magic product, and the weight-gain people show you how cheap and easy it is to provide pleasure to yourself via your tongue. Few seem concerned with providing you more than a short-term quick-fix.

Are you a little upset? Many of us are allowing ourselves to be used. In a sense, the journey to lose weight is partly the journey to become an adult, to see our culture for what it is and to choose how we interact with it, what we absorb, how we spend our hard-earned dollars — not simply to react, soak up whatever comes, and spend to soothe.

Consider your own attitude toward overweight people. I bet you promote acceptance. I bet that you believe that all people are worthwhile, no matter how they look. And yet, I also bet that you're doing whatever you can to either stay thin or lose weight. I bet you look in mirrors and evaluate yourself all the time. I bet you look at others and in a flash, before you even consciously know what you're doing, judge them. Look, we all do this to some degree. Let's be honest about it.

Why are there anorexic girls and boys and men and women in hospitals having liquid sugar dripped into their veins? Why have stomach stapling and liposuction become routine surgeries? Do you think these people are so different from you and me? Do you think their emotional issues are so different from ours? Can you see how so many of our knee-jerk reactions and serious psychological issues are sourced in the energy of marketing, advertising, and the culture of thin?

Look around you and see how our culture tells us, "You're not beautiful enough to drive this car. You're not thin enough to wear these clothes. You're not hot enough to feel sexy or confident. You're not enough. You're not enough. You're not enough." Consume enough of this and soon the message is playing in our heads all day long. Then, before we know it, we're good little consumers, spending time and money and energy to make ourselves thin, fashionable, and beautiful on the outside, hoping that will make us acceptable and lovable on the inside. We mistake the packaging for the product and apply that abusive standard to ourselves and everyone around us.

The journey toward physical health is a spiritual path. Self-acceptance, self-love, and compassion for ourselves and others are easier when we realize that even though we can be so quick to judge, part of that judgment reflex has been taught to us by the cultural marketing and selling machine. Consuming less of this, choosing more carefully what we put into our brains, eases our spiritual path and makes choosing what we put into our mouths a little easier.

chapter 12
Do **YOU** Have
an **EATING DISORDER?**

There are more eating disorders than we're willing to admit. Most people that are overweight or suffer from bulimia or anorexia are aware of their disorder. Many of the rest of us, however, live in a socially accepted bubble of denial. It's just that there are so many of us in the bubble, when we look around and compare habits, what we do seems normal.

In fact, what we call eating disorders are really a small piece of the overall picture. For example, we don't refer to heart disease as an eating disorder, but how do we think our arteries get clogged? We don't refer to type II diabetes as an eating disorder, but how do we think our pancreas gets overworked? How many of the diseases that happen to us when we're sixty and seventy happen because of our eating habits when we're thirty, forty, and fifty?

If I'm scaring you a little, I apologize. On the one hand, I really want to help you to see that small differences now make big differences down the road. On the other hand, the challenge can seem so great that I understand how even thinking about adjusting your eating habits can feel like kicking out one of your legs from underneath you. However, I believe that the truth will set you free. It did for me. Thus, I'm going to call a spade a spade. If you have the courage to tell the truth about your eating habits, I honor you. If you can't right now, I honor you. We each have to follow our own path and come out of the closet at our own pace.

First, let's define *order* before we explore eating *disorder*. Healthful eating, I believe, is where you eat nutritious foods in proportion with the physical demands of your body. You have an accurate understanding about yourself, your habits, what you need in terms of fuel, and on what schedule. You've learned good judgment about healthy food choices. You're in tune with your body, knowing when you're hungry and when you're full.

If this all seems like a lot of work, it is. But the payoffs of healthy eating are undeniable. Your energy levels are higher and more consistent all day long. You cope better with stress and adversity. You need less caffeine to wake up and less alcohol to calm down. Your internal organs are less stressed. You have fewer health problems, fewer doctor's visits, fewer pills to take. Simply, you feel better. You sleep better. You do your job better. You're able to end your workday with energy left over for other pursuits, relationships, children. In short, eating habits that are "in order" create a positive cycle that impacts the whole of your life.

It is a big mountain to climb, but the journey is worth it. Where are you on your journey?

- Do you avoid eating all day long so you can eat (and drink) more at night?
- When you're alone in the house, do you eat your comfort food, like a pound of bacon or a pint of ice cream or half a pizza?
- Do you binge on health food?
- Do you have a kitchen stocked with comfort foods?
- Do you eat to make yourself feel better?
- Do you keep eating even when you're full?
- Do you munch or snack on whatever's around?

- Do you eat when you're bored?
- Do you hide food?
- Do you eat in secret?
- Do you lie about what you eat or how much you eat?
- Do you feel guilty about your eating habits?
- Does your weight yo-yo up and down?
- Do you eat more when you're with your family?
- Does your weight go up five to ten pounds over the holidays?
- Do you know what kind of fat is in your food?
- Do you devour the restaurant breadbasket like the stock market's about to crash?
- Do you save a quarter pound of grandma's fudge, or some other sugary snack, to handle relationship stress?
- Do you go from one fad diet to the next?
- Do you plan your next meal while you're still eating your current one?
- Do you chew your food?
- Do you eat on automatic pilot, "waking up" at the end of a meal and realizing you forgot to taste your food?
- Do you skip meals so you can fit into an outfit?

- Do you "eat good" some days so you can be "bad" on other days?

Part of the reason it's so difficult to really see the way we abuse food is because we're aware, at some level, of how hard it is to change our eating habits. We're busy enough and stressed enough as it is without trying to climb that mountain. We figure that eating healthily is how top athletes function optimally and isn't really necessary for the rest of us. We're just trying to stay (or become) thin enough to fit into our clothes, thin enough to feel okay about being naked.

However, we are all top athletes in our own way. Each of us is running a very personal, very important race, and we each deserve to do more than function — we deserve to function optimally. Acknowledge the truth of your eating habits and begin the journey toward your best self.

chapter 13

The Passive-Aggressive Martyrs Society (PAMS)

There is something wonderful about giving. Contributing to someone else's life can create a cycle of good karma that often comes back around, and part of living a meaningful life is understanding how our lives are of service to others. And yet....

How many of us really give from a whole and complete place within ourselves? How often is giving to another really a method of getting something for ourselves?

It is a truth of human nature that many of us aren't raised to be ourselves. We're raised to be who our parents want us to be or who are parents wish themselves to be. Our parents did the best they could, but inevitably there are wounds that lurk deep within. To compound the challenge we must contend with our materialistic, acquisitive, fast-paced, often spiritually and emotionally superficial culture. The result of this is that as children many of us feel that in order to survive we must become what other people expect.

The amazing thing is, when we're young, we're often right. Many of us do have to become what others want us to be in order to avoid punishment, to belong, to feel safe within our inner circles. In other words, abandoning ourselves works. We please our parents, we please our teachers, and as we grow older, we learn how to be what our friends and family members need — but we still haven't learned how to be ourselves. Our method of surviving childhood has become an adult way of life.

Those of us who identify ourselves as "giving" people are frequently also chameleon-like. We have the ability to be with different groups of people and often have different groups of friends. We especially like to have one-on-one time, where conversations resemble therapy sessions because they're so emotional and cathartic. Part of this is because we know how to be what someone else needs. We can feel the other person's point of view. We step into their shoes. We empathize with their issues. And so we become the sounding board, the dumping ground, advice giver, and all-around problem solver.

Meanwhile, our own authentic self is locked away and we continue to die inside. This is why spending time with certain friends or family can be so exhausting. Not only are we taking on their problems, not only are we being chameleons who adjust to meet their needs, we're feeling profound loneliness while we muster the strength to conceal our feelings. It's tiring.

The kernel of this behavior is really quite compassionate and rooted in genuine empathy. However, it is also why PAMS so often get into codependent relationships. We easily become enablers. PAMS are often amateur therapists who believe that without the long phone calls at midnight, without the constant emails, without all the handholding and encouragement, the frail psyches of our friends would fall apart.

The reality is often the opposite. There is a limit to how much you can help someone. Frequently the only thing you can do, the best thing you can do, is to let them have the dignity of their own struggle, their own journey. It is a truth of this life that while we all need support and love and encouragement, lessons must be learned on our own.

PAMS can have such loving and compassionate natures, such deep empathy, and this is why it's so tragic to watch us abuse it. Often, we don't use our compassion toward ourselves. We don't love ourselves. We seek out people who need us, situations where we can be indispensable. We assume the role of host, counselor, protector, and we do it to distract ourselves. It's an addiction. We hold many of our friends and family members hostage to our needs, then use them for our own gratification. We don't allow them to meet their own challenges or solve their own problems because we need their problems to have something to do and to feel helpful, useful, validated, and appreciated.

Thus, our caring natures are co-opted by our pattern of abandoning ourselves, and so we become martyrs. We put everyone else's needs ahead of our own. If someone asks how we are, we might answer with our friend's problems: "I'm fine, but Sally's going through a divorce, that's been really hard. My mom's thinking of quitting her job because of her boss, and my friend Misty's health problems are just out of control, so I've got a lot on my plate right now." After we spend time with friends who are going through difficult situations, we don't just feel compassion, we feel what they're feeling! And even later that day, we're still vibrating with their emotions.

Being a martyr is like that. We continue to give our energy and time and emotions long after the moment has passed. We've sacrificed ourselves, as martyrs do. What are our needs? Do we have time for exercise? For meditation? Gardening, music, a TV show? Often, we're not sure. We feel the problems of our friends and family and our children. We're dealing with their divorce or alcoholism or financial insecurity or unpopularity at school. We use the struggles of others to make our own issues seem tiny and insignificant. We welcome the needs of others to live inside of us because we've made space by sacrificing and suppressing our own needs. Just as when we were children, our authentic selves live deep within, crying out, but not getting our attention.

One outcome of our martyrdom is feeling extremely resentful. For starters, PAMS take care of others because, in part, we want to show them how we'd like to be taken care of. But they never care for us in the way we'd like. So we're pouring love and time and attention down what feels like a black hole, unconsciously expecting that down the road at some point we'll receive the same in return, which we never do (and if we do, it's never enough). We think we give from a pure place of altruism, with no strings attached, but as soon as the other person lets us down, we explode with resentments. We immediately know all of the things we've done for them across time. It's like a scorecard jumps into our heads and we're thinking, how could she do that to me, after all I've done for her!

Much of the time, it's a game only being played by us. The game is: do really nice things for people (without being asked), then hold them to a debt they don't even know they have… and, oh, never ask for anything you really need directly. Instead, sacrifice yourself in order to control how others feel about you and how they behave toward you and try to get your needs met that way. Only, it doesn't work so well, does it? It's like secretly slipping twenty dollars into someone's pocket and then getting pissed when they don't pay you back. A true PAM, of course, will give away their last twenty dollars and then get even more incensed when their sacrifice isn't appreciated.

The reality is that we resent ourselves. We've abandoned ourselves and we project that onto another person. When they don't pay us our twenty dollars, when they don't care for us the way we've cared for them, we think that they've abandoned us. This is why PAMs are people who can like someone for a long time and then all of a sudden, because of one event, completely change their mind. It's because resentments get stored for a long time and then explode all at once.

That was me, "Suffering in Silence," "Bitter but Breathing," all the while resentful inside for never being appreciated but never choosing to appreciate myself first. That really had never occurred to me as an option — for me to put me first, to appreciate me first. No, I was determined to make myself indispensable to you so that you could never discard me and throw me away. And, if I could be everything that you needed for me to be for you, I could always covertly control how you felt about me. Sneaky, huh? But it was survival, and it was all that I knew at the time. Thank God for consciousness. Now I relish being able to take care of me first. Now I can truly be there for other people when I so choose.

How often do you simply say thank you when someone gives you a compliment? There was a time when I couldn't. It's a funny thing, but PAMs, who are so desperately in need of being seen in a positive light, reject anything positive that comes their way. PAMs feel unworthy of a compliment. We have identities dedicated to feeling broken on the inside. There's no room for feeling good about ourselves. There's no place for a compliment to land. There's no room for anyone to love us. The idea of really being seen, heard, and loved threatens to overwhelm us at our core with a tidal wave of complex emotions.

Furthermore, we don't want to owe anyone anything. When other people give to us, even the gift of a compliment, we think there are strings attached, and we want to know what they want from us. Of course, much of the time we're projecting — we're the ones who give with strings attached, and so we imagine that everyone else is doing the same. We're suspicious of people and their motivations for doing good, even though we hold ourselves up as selfless givers with no agenda. Red flag, anyone?

PAM behavior, in the long term, doesn't work. But it sure does in the short term. We achieve social standing. We do become indispensable, perhaps at home, perhaps at work. We belong in almost any group of people. It certainly feels as though we're making a difference in other people's lives, and sometimes perhaps we are. However, without discovering our true selves, we are (at best) a hollow shell, one devoted to giving on the outside and to denial on the inside. It's a lonely existence that so many wonderful and empathic people are living — and it's a great opportunity for these same people to bloom and flower and step into their full potential.

The path is quite simple, yet not easy. It's the same no matter what your issue is, whether you're a PAM or not. It's a way of life.

Here it is. Be. See. Feel. Be. See. Feel. Be... You get the idea, but let's look a bit more closely.

Be yourself. In this moment. Be who you are, not who you'd like to be, not who you're supposed to be, but simply yourself, as you exist right... now. If you need to or want to, give yourself permission to be a PAM, to be a big PAM, to give and give and give to the limit of your capacity.

See yourself. As you are being yourself, notice who that is. The more you become aware of your situation, the more you are able to get real with yourself about why you do the things you do, the more interesting thoughts and feelings will come bubbling up from below. What are the payoffs for your behavior? How have you set things up to be the way they are?

Feel your feelings. Feel the need to give. Feel the threat of a compliment. Feel the loneliness at the dinner table. Feel the energy it takes to do the happy dance. Feel your own inner neediness. Feel the discomfort when you think you "owe" someone. Feel the deep sadness within. You've got to feel it to move through it.

Be, see, and feel. This is the process by which our

authentic self gains expression. Like a small neglected child, our true nature needs our time, our attention, and our compassion. Feeling those painful, powerful feelings is like holding that little boy or girl in our lap and rocking them while they cry. Avoiding those feelings is like ignoring the child.

How would you treat a crying child? Would you ignore them or care for them? Your inner child needs this attention, this gentle compassion, and only you can provide it. The best part is, the more you give to yourself, the more you can truly give to others.

chapter 14
SELF-CELEBRATION

Masturbation is a metaphor for life. When you masturbate, you give yourself what you want. Why not do that in other areas of life?

In exercise, you can celebrate yourself. Ask your body what it wants and listen. Then, simply move accordingly. Eating, too, can be a self-celebration. So can breathing.

For years I never knew that it was okay for me to celebrate myself. Giving to myself seemed selfish, and what would people think about that? But I realized my life needed balance and I had to stop all my mad doingness. So I began to think about all the things that bring me great joy, ways to honor and nurture myself — massages, game nights, prayer, date nights with my partner, calls with my coach, vacations, exercise, rest, meditation, and more. I discovered that by celebrating my-self first, others around me felt permission to celebrate themselves as well. And by celebrating myself, I get to celebrate others with so much more unconditional love.

Can you find a job or create work for yourself that is a celebration of who you are? Can you be in a relation-ship where you each celebrate the truth of the other? What nurtures you? What fills your heart?

Our lives are truly full of opportunities for pleasure. Treat yourself.

chapter 15
EVERY CELL Is a MIRACULOUS MACHINE

Exercise is an opportunity to feel your body in the present moment and relate to it with compassion and understanding. This is an ongoing spiritual relationship with considerable real-world consequences. Do you want your body to work when you're sixty? Do you want to be able to walk up a flight of stairs? Carry bags of groceries? Dance? Play with grandchildren? Have passionate sex?

We plan financially for our retirement, we pay into IRAs and Social Security, but do we strive to be stronger, healthier, and more fit as we age? Why not? After all, what good is the money we've saved if we're not healthy enough to enjoy it?

Many of us do not exercise regularly. Our bodies want to move. When they don't, they get cranky. Muscles atrophy and get a little tighter. You're a little more stiff in the morning; there's a little more pain at night. It's a little harder to get in and out of your car or your desk chair. Your joints creak. Your clothes are tight. You can't lift your laundry basket. You buy ibuprofen more regularly.

Some of us only learn to appreciate our bodies when they're taken away from us — taken quickly. A broken leg, a slipped disc, paralysis, chemotherapy — any of these can keep you in bed for several weeks and make you appreciate simple things like dressing yourself or being able to walk. However, many of us are allowing our bodies to slip away slowly. We lose a little more mobility and get a little weaker each year. We put on a little more weight. We require more of our organs and our joints. We become more vulnerable to disease. In a sense, we're like the frog in the pot of water. If you toss a frog into a pot of boiling water, he'll jump right out. If you put him in cool water and heat it slowly to boiling, he'll let himself be cooked to death.

We need to think differently about exercise. We need to approach it differently too. The idea that exercise is something we do in order to look like the hard-bodies on magazine covers is undermining us. The idea that exercise is something we do in order to become thin and beautiful, to stop our thighs from jiggling, or to fit into our skinny clothes is crippling us. The idea that exercise makes us more likely to meet our future mate? Killing us.

Think about your relationship with a friend, relative, or partner. You enjoy each other's company. You make conversation. You play games with each other. It's fun, right? It's the same with exercise. *When you exercise, you are in relationship with yourself.* You acknowledge the truth of how the body feels. You listen to what the body wants. Then, you empathize and begin a very intimate dialogue, a conversation with the body... called exercise.

Here's the secret ingredient: fun. You must have fun. You may have committed to exercising three times a week, bought new workout clothes, renewed your gym membership, and made specific time in your schedule. But if you want to keep your word to yourself, exercise must be a "get-to" not a "have-to."

Everyone that figures out how to have fun through exercise is successful because fun is self-sustaining. Sure, occasionally I have to apply a little willpower to get myself started, get into my gym clothes and running shoes, but most of the time it's something I get to do — not something I have to do.

For me, exercise is my meditation time. I know other people who use it creatively and bring a notebook to the gym. Some people read or watch TV or escape into their own mixes on CD or iPod. Some like to be social and go to a yoga or pole dancing class, and some like to teach themselves to rollerblade. Be creative and figure out your own way.

Consider your eyes — we're used to having them so it's easy to take our vision for granted. To take our bodies for granted. To take our lives for granted. However, each of our lives is important. Each of our bodies is incredible. Exercise, aside from being fun and healthful, is a gesture of gratitude. It's a way of saying thank you for all the simple miracles we experience daily.

chapter 16
LET GO of the
NEED to Be RIGHT

Right answers are comforting. When we're right, we feel safe. This is why so many arguments, fights, and wars start over people defending the rightness of their ideas. Consider the rift between Democrats and Republicans. Yes, it's partly about power and greed, but fundamentally these two parties disagree about how to lead the country. This disagreement could be valuable to all Americans if each party was genuinely curious about the other's view. They would find common ground. They would investigate each other's opinions, build consensus, and make the best decisions they could with the information they have.

But that's not what happens, is it? No, each party strives to blame the other for mistakes, take credit for victories, and prove that their way of doing things is "right." Rather than guiding the country using common sense, our leaders have chosen to fight about who has the "right" system for doing things, the "right" leaders, the "right" platform of beliefs. Why? The gridlock is evident. Our government is inefficient. So why do politicians insist on maintaining this political culture?

It's because of us, voters and non-voters. I don't mean that not enough of us vote, or that we elect the wrong people. My point is that we — all of us — need to be right. We need to feel like the country is moving in the "right" direction. We want to know that the policies made by the current administration will be "right." We wouldn't feel very safe going to sleep at night if the president gave the State of the Union and said, "You know, the world is really complicated and there's a lot we don't know. We can barely predict the weather more than a few days in advance. We can't predict the stock market. We certainly can't predict local, national, or world politics. But we're doing the best we can with the information we have."

No, we want to hear that we're the good guys and that our problems can be blamed on the bad guys. We want to know that the plan the president is talking about is the "right" plan, the best plan, the one where the good guys win quickly and taxes don't go up and nobody dies in the process.

I chose that example because many of us may not care so much about politics. In the grand scheme, there are more important things to think about, right? We've got personal crises, situations at work, relationship issues — we're busy. Now, consider how unimportant politics is to the totality of your existence, and then consider the strength of your opinions. You probably vote one way or another all the time. You probably have friends and family who vote the same way. You probably can't date people who have different political views.

Interesting, isn't it? We're not political experts. We don't care to know all the relevant history, all the details of every policy, all the background on each candidate, and yet we still care passionately about our political opinions. Why? Why not just vote the way we vote and watch how it all shakes out? Why do we have to be so invested in being right?

Here's why: we're so invested, we care so much, because we need to be right about *everything*, including politics. First, we want to be right about the world and how it works. We've each got a theory of human nature, of why people do the things they do, why the world keeps spinning around. Some of us have highly developed scientific explanations. Some use religion. Some use their own observations of the world. Few of us, however, admit that we just don't know why the world is the way it is.

We also have a desperate need to be right about who we are. For years I fought to be right because being right for me meant that I was loveable, worthy, safe, protected, and powerful. As a child, being wrong meant upheaval, disappointment, vulnerability, and annihilation. I held onto being right in fear of ever allowing my heart to feel that level of devastation. I never wanted to feel that level of hurt again, and I never wanted anybody to have anything over me in fear of feeling that depth of angst, confusion, and destruction. I so needed to be seen, heard, gotten, and loved. I am so grateful that I no longer have anything to prove to myself, that *I* see me, hear me, get me, and love me first.

We will defend our nature and our opinions practically to the death because we believe that we are our thoughts, feelings, bodies, and egos. Why do battered wives stay with their abusive husbands? Why do people stay in jobs they don't like — without searching for a new job? Why do we have trouble making changes of any kind?

It's because we're all afraid to leave the known world for the perils of the unknown. Better the devil we know than the devil we don't, we think. Therefore, we enslave ourselves to consistency. We do our best to stay the same. We compliment each other that way: "It's been such a long time... and you haven't changed a bit." We prize consistency in our leaders: "I've voted the same way on this for twenty-five years." We watch TV shows where the whole idea is for the characters to encounter a situation every week that produces no real change — because we want to see the same characters next week.

It's no surprise that we have a tremendous need for consistency because we live in a world that is constantly transforming. However, rather than responding to the dynamic and changing nature of the world with fear, rather than promoting a policy of consistency at all costs, try responding with courage.

Courage means the courage to not know. To not define yourself ahead of time, not assume that you know who you will be tomorrow, how you will think, what you will feel. Identifying and pursuing your dreams requires courage, as does accepting who you truly are in this moment and trusting yourself to handle whatever may come.

You can't have your dream and stay the same. To stay consistent, you must resist learning. You must refuse to confront obstacles or new situations. You must avoid experience. Consider your past. You can probably see many changes you've made along the way, many you did not expect. Now consider your future — are you trying to keep it predictable? Same as the present, only richer, thinner, safer, better?

You wouldn't be reading this book if you didn't have a positive agenda for growth. My suggestion to you is that you will find more satisfaction in this process if you can let go of the need to be right about who you are and who you need to be. This means letting go of attachments to opinions, labels, beliefs, and patterns. Replace these attachments with wonder in the moment. Wonder about who you are, who you will be, and have faith in your process. This is a courageous stance from which you can fulfill your heart's desires.

chapter 17
WHAT Do You WANT?

Achieving goals is not equal to living an exceptional life — this is undeniable. Look at people who have achieved so many of the goals that society deems important — people who are thin, attractive, wealthy, smart, famous, powerful, stylish, respected. Many of these individuals do not feel happy or fulfilled.

This is scary because many of us envy these people. We operate under the fantasy that, if we could just do more, we would get more, and if we had more, then we would be more, and then we would feel better and live better lives. But this just isn't true. There are people who have great material wealth and feel miserable. There are people living at the poverty line who feel happy and fulfilled. The simple fact is that achieving goals only makes us feel better temporarily.

Achievement can be an addiction. First we generate lots of adrenaline in order to complete our important tasks. The adrenaline and the tasks are a magnificent and socially approved method of distracting ourselves from how we really feel. Really busy people are productive citizens, good Americans. Then again, many of these productive citizens are heavy drinkers. Workaholism is no better or worse than alcoholism, and strangely enough, many people are both workaholics and alcoholics. This is because any addiction is sourced in concealing and denying painful feelings. Tasks and goals, like alcohol, can serve the same purpose.

Outcomes and tasks are about DOING. Living life is about BEING. Thus, a high-quality life is one that emphasizes process, not results — the journey, not the destination; the present, not the future.

A goal, therefore, is an outcome that provides direction for the journey that is your life. The question is, *are the goals you've chosen congruent with a journey you enjoy?*

Many of us choose goals that are designed to get someone else to love us. We choose goals that, if achieved, would make up for wounds from the past. We choose goals out of fear, anger, or revenge. These goals lead us exactly where we need to go. They lead us to experiences that challenge us to accept ourselves and become more authentic, present, and conscious. This may mean having experiences that feel uncomfortable, stifling, and impossible — because that's what it takes to get us to consider whether we're walking our own path or the paths others have laid out for us. The truth is that waking up can be a bitch.

To speed your process, however, let me explain where so many people get stuck: forgiveness. Forgiving is an act that releases other people's energy from your life. When you forgive another person, you don't exonerate them or excuse their behavior or invite them to dinner. It's not about them — forgiveness is about you, for you. You choose to let your anger toward them go, to accept what's done as done, and to move on with your life because that's what takes care of you best.

Forgiveness often becomes easier when you have more information. It can be difficult to forgive your parents for decisions they made or actions they took when you were a child or teenager. However, if you could find out what their childhood and teenage years were like, if you could imagine what it must have been like for them to be who they were during your most impressionable years, you may find the compassion and understanding you need to forgive them. If not, that's okay. Your parents can run your life even if they aren't alive as long as you make decisions to show them you're worthy, gain their love, get their attention, or prove to them they shouldn't have neglected you.

It can be hard to forgive parents, friends, an ex, or a spouse, but the toughest person to forgive is you. We all demand so much of ourselves, especially when it comes to weighing and measuring our lives, especially when it comes to goals and achievements. Can you forgive yourself for being imperfect? Can you forgive yourself for your past, for your history? Can you forgive yourself for being unable to forgive?

Forgiveness has set me free in more ways than I could have ever imagined, but most importantly, I've learned to forgive myself. I forgive myself for not being perfect, and have learned that my imperfections are absolutely my perfection. Hence, I am perfect exactly as I am. We all are.

In a sense, forgiveness is a threshold one must cross to become an adult. As children, we're taught a lot about the world and how to interact with it. At a certain point, however, we realize that there's a lot of misinformation in what we've learned and how we've interpreted it. Naturally, we rebel. Rebellion creates space in which we can grow and discover who we really are. Unfortunately, many of us remain in these first two phases — we either continue to buy into the world we were taught about as children, or we rebel against that world. But the next level, the level of the adult, is where we determine for ourselves who we are and the world in which we live. The key to walking your own path is forgiveness. Forgive those you perceive as enemies. Forgive people from your past. Forgive yourself for who you used to be and embrace who you are. This makes it possible for you to align your goals with your true self and fill your life with the meaning and fulfillment you deserve.

chapter 18
THE ONE

The One is not a person. He or she is a figment of your imagination, a projection into the future, a fantasy. The One is not someone you date, he's a list of qualities you look for in the people you audition. The One is an obstacle to getting married, not an accurate picture of Mr. Right.

Our culture puts so much pressure on us to get married, especially on women. Then there's the biological clock on top of all the societal pressure. The truth is that in some way, you're playing beat the clock. You're probably a lot more desperate to find The One than you're willing to admit.

The question is, do you want to get married or do you want relief from your desperation? Getting married will not solve or eliminate your desperation, but dealing with your desperation will make it much more likely that you'll get married. In other words, getting married is common. Staying married is not. Completeness, fulfillment, wholeness, and safety need to be looked for and found within. Getting married is not about finding the guy or girl — it's about finding you.

"Relationships are not to make you happy, but to make you conscious," says Eckhart Tolle, and the marriage relationship is no exception. A spouse is not an end but a means to an end — in this case, a means to your growth, your awareness, your consciousness. When you understand this, you stop interviewing people to see if they will fulfill your needs and you start appreciating people for what you learn about yourself when you're with them.

The ache in your heart isn't for your soulmate. It's for the neglected parts of your own soul. No One can heal your wounds and make you whole — except for you.

chapter 19
PLAYDATES

First dates, for most of us, are stressful. We have that awkward feeling of being evaluated while we pretend not to evaluate the other person. We experience the disappointment of unsatisfied expectations and the fear of developing an intimate connection that, if broken, would break and shred our heart. In fact, as dating becomes more important to us, the fun can disappear.

Remember playdates? When you were a kid and you got stuffed in a car and taken to some other house to play with another kid? You didn't really have expectations, you were going to make up the fun as you went along. You were just going to play. That's what a date should be — a playdate.

When you go out on a date, you are either an invitation or a life sentence. If you have expectations, if you're comparing the other person to The One in your head, you might as well make your judgment, bang your gavel, and find them prison clothes that fit. But on a playdate, you bring a sense of adventure. You're present in the moment. That's what an invitation is — a chance to play a new game in a new moment with a new person.

The problem is that we frequently have to play the same game and repeat the same patterns, over and over and over. We get the same lesson until the lesson is learned. This is what "your type," is. Your type is your type of lesson, not just your weakness for tall, dark, and handsome. In short, most of us are literally stuck in a pattern of dating people who trigger our issues!

Welcome to the world. The relationship roller coaster is inevitable. The sun comes up in the morning, the pope is Catholic, and you will have rocky moments in your relationships. The question is, are you going to deny that the problems exist or are you going to be aware of them so you can learn?

Give yourself permission to judge your dates and only go out with those people who fit your criteria. Give yourself permission to not be over your last relationship or to try to cure your post-break-up malaise with another relationship. Allow yourself the permission to go on a bad date. Go on several! All I ask is that you notice how you feel throughout these experiences. Once you've felt how unfulfilling it is to judge and be judged, to allow previous relationships to control you, or to go on bad dates, you'll stop. But only once you've *felt* it. Good judgment evolves through experience.

Part of good judgment is knowing that everyone's not for you, and you're not for everyone. Give yourself permission to say, "No thanks." You never have to give someone your phone number! Give yourself permission to say, "Let's call it a night," at any time. You never have to grit your teeth and endure a bad date! Everyone's not for you, and you're not for everyone!

Remember, there's no way to protect yourself from the pain of relationships. If you accept that as a given, it becomes easier to appreciate the joyous moments along the way. If you see relationships as opportunities to learn, you'll find humor in the low moments. You're going to be on the roller coaster anyway. Give yourself permission to ride the ride.

In my mid-thirties, after the break-up of a twelve-year relationship, I put myself back on the ride. I decided that I was going to put myself out there (with no agenda) and just have fun. And I really did it. I met people for coffee (which I don't even drink), lunches, dinners, brunches, beach dates, and dancing. I gave myself the permission to experience as much as I could that felt right for me. "Fifty dates" became my motto. I'm sure that I had well over fifty dates, but it was never about the number, it was all about putting myself back out there and getting back up on the horse.

Out of that willingness, I met some wonderful people and had some amazing experiences. (Okay, I had some not so amazing experiences too — but that's another book.) But because I had no ulterior motives, those dates were allowed to be just that — experiences. I got to know some extraordinary people and learn tons about myself. Once that muscle was worked, I stopped dating the masses and began to date only people that I felt were potential relationship material for me. I truly let it go and invited the love of my life (in meditation, intention, visualization, and prayer) to join me for the rest of my life.

You, however, may prefer to stick to traditional dating. It can be complicated, but if you prefer traditional dating, great! Bring your expectations and lists, have a mutual audition, and notice what happens. People find each other in all sorts of ways, and if you find someone whose list looks like you and your list looks like them, congratulations. If that doesn't happen, that's okay.

You can try again when you're ready. Maybe change a few items on your list, or burn it and try playdating.

The advantage of playdating is that most dates can be really fun. When you leave your expectations at the door, you're less likely to feel disappointed. Usually, after a few less-than-perfect experiences, people using the traditional dating method have to take some time to themselves to recover from their disappointment. But if a playdate goes "badly" and you feel bittersweet, you can set up a new date and wash, rinse, repeat. Not only will you probably have fun, but it's likely you will learn something valuable about yourself.

And then, when you've let go of your fantasy of The One, when you've stopped judging and are just getting out there and having a good time… someone great will come along….

chapter 20
UNTIL DEATH DO US PART
(Unless It's Really Not Working)

Your wedding is a symbol of who you are and the marriage to come.

- Are you an equal partner?
- Are you a dictator or a bridezilla?
- Is your wedding about expressing love, or more about satisfying traditions and conventions?
- Can you accommodate each other's needs without being resentful?
- Are you inviting the people you truly want to be there, or are you fulfilling social and familial obligations?

- Are you both involved, or is one of you driving and one of you sleeping in the backseat?
- Is the wedding going to cost as much as you make in a year, and would you rather put some of that toward a house or a college education?
- Is the goal of the ceremony to impress others and make a statement to society, or is it to honor yourselves and the sacredness of your union?
- Are you having the wedding in a church because religion is important to you and because you want to raise your children by a certain doctrine, or is it to placate religious members of your family?
- Is your wedding a reflection of the essence of your relationship, a statement about what and who you value, or is it a carefully choreographed dance to fulfill a fantasy?

Many brides see their wedding day as the day that's all about them. Many grooms see their wedding day as being about everything but them. This is a reflection of stereotypes, that a woman's whole job is to marry and have kids, and that when a man settles down it's like climbing into a cage. Some weddings are a reflection of the political and social needs of the two sets of parents — especially if they're the ones paying.

Remember, your wedding is a symbol of who you are and the marriage to come. The intentions you hold in your heart as you go through this process are what make a wedding such a powerful ritual. If you're trying to achieve a fantasy wedding, you may be trying to achieve a fantasy relationship. If you're allowing stereotypes and traditions and the needs of others to determine your choices, that's the tone you set for the years ahead.

One aspect of the wedding that doesn't receive enough attention is the planning and preparation. Sure, people plan every detail, but that's usually because they want to create an outcome, not enjoy or learn from a process. This is especially important because, say it with me now: *my wedding is a symbol of who I am and my marriage to come.* The planning stages will teach you about yourself and each other. You'll learn to communicate better, accommodate each other, and even compromise. You'll ask for what you want, listen to what your partner wants, and enjoy the process of working on something together — the definition of a great marriage.

Some marriages end in divorce. There are, of course, many reasons for that. Sexual chemistry can be misleading. Parents and friends often have agendas that do not coincide with our own. For many of us, marriage is a ritual that almost feels required by our religion. Most importantly, however, we fear being alone, so we tie the knot to make sure that we never will be.

There can be a lot of pressure applied to what is fundamentally an intimate partnership, not a much-awaited social event. Thus, while divorce is extremely not fun, it can be better than the alternative — a relationship based in suffering, survival, or desperation.

Imagine two people sailing a boat in high winds. It capsizes. They flounder in the water until a piece of driftwood passes by. They grab it; it's just big enough for both of them to use as a raft. For many people, this is marriage — in a state of mutual desperation, people hang onto each other.

Suppose our two sailors drift for a few days and then wash up on an island, but they don't leave the raft. For many people, this is marriage: hanging onto the raft, bobbing in the shallow water near the beach, continuing to expose themselves to the elements, and risking slow internal deterioration.

You see, leaving the raft means that the forces that brought the sailors together won't be there anymore. Leaving the raft means to risk being lonely. This is the truest and most powerful drive to partnership, the discomfort of feeling lonely. The catch is that partnership only alleviates the discomfort in the short term.

The fantasy of partnership sourced in mutual desperation becomes more problematic when the marriage commitment is layered on top. A wedding is sanctioned by the State, possibly ritualized by religion, and witnessed by friends and family. For many people, this is marriage: a short-term antidote to loneliness and a long-term effort to keep our tax breaks, be welcome in our churches, and maintain the respect of our loved ones.

The true antidote to loneliness is not marriage, but faith. When you walk with a Higher Power you are never alone. This makes a long-lasting and fulfilling partnership possible. Remember, your wedding is a symbol of who you are and your marriage to come. Have you grounded your union in your spiritual and emotional truth?

Notice yourself as you go toward the altar. Are you being who you want to be? Are you seeing the people around you as they are in this moment? Are you kicking off your marriage with a day of fantasy? Do you have the courage to source your relationship in reality and surprise yourself with how magical and extraordinary a wedding can be?

chapter 21
THE SEX CONNECTION

Sex is an activity designed to create connection. Yes, for fun, and yes, for procreation, but in today's world sex is also an opportunity to deepen trust, to explore emotions, to surrender to the moment and be completely vulnerable.

Have you ever heard someone say, "They *knew* each other — in the biblical sense?" That's because the ancient Hebrew word for *sex* was the same as "to know." Who gets to know you?

The journey to great sex with a particular partner is like the journey to a great body or a great relationship or a great life. It takes twists and turns, adventures, and lessons. After all, there's so much of who we are as individuals tied up in our sexuality — it only makes sense that sex would challenge us to grow emotionally and spiritually and impact the rest of our lives as well.

What turns you on? What turns your partner on? Exploration of your tastes and desires is an adventure you and your partner deserve to share. Give yourself permission to think outside the box. Discover new positions, be creative; even give the magazine tips a whirl. Just remember that the basics always apply — can you give with an open heart? Can you receive pleasure openly and rejoice in being alive? Can you know another and let them know you moment by precious moment?

Sex is a form of conversation. Whether we're talking with our voices or our bodies or both, we're connected to the extent that we are authentic, vulnerable. Thus, the key to great sex is the willingness to risk being yourself, being seen as yourself, and being loved as yourself. Conversation can be a profound experience — in bed and out of bed.

chapter 22
PREVENTING AFFAIRS

If you want to preserve the sanctity of your relationship and prevent affairs, there is one true solution: you must work on yourself. Both partners in any relationship play a role in any infidelity. Yes, someone makes the choice to go outside the relationship, but red flags are always happening long before the actual affair takes place.

Both people involved have the chance to notice the emotional disconnection that can lead to physical infidelity. Both people have the opportunity to communicate honestly and openly with each other. Both people can opt for counseling or life coaching for any reason long before commitments are broken. So by the time you or your partner is having an affair, you're both responsible. Still, you can only be accountable for yourself. Therefore, the best way to prevent affairs is to develop your consciousness and authenticity.

When someone has an affair, it usually means there's something they want from the relationship that they're not getting, like feeling special or beautiful or sexy or validated. However, most of what we seek in relationships we also seek within ourselves. What we can't find within we search for in our partner or in our relationship, and when it's no longer there, we look for another partner. We do this until we learn to find what we're looking for where it actually is — inside ourselves.

An affair isn't good or bad. It just is. It can be a means to end an abusive, horrific relationship. It can be a wake-up call, a reminder about what's good between you and your partner. It can begin a process of spring cleaning, removing skeletons from closets and invigorating a relationship. It can also be, and probably more frequently is, a spectacular debacle sourced in miscommunication and unconsciousness that contributes to the pain and suffering of everyone involved.

I see an affair as an opportunity that I don't need. I prefer to be in a committed relationship that works for me. To that end, I work with an extraordinary life coach, because, say it with me now, *the best way to prevent me or my partner from having an affair is to develop myself.*

I also check in with my partner often. Mostly we just talk and enjoy each other's company, but occasionally a check-in allows us to catch something early. The red flags that indicate a relationship is off track are unique to every individual and can change over time. Some people spend more time at the office to stay out of the house. For others, working harder shows commitment to the shared goals of the relationship. Some people have sex less frequently because of an emotional disconnect. Some people have sex more frequently when they don't want to talk with each other. Don't assume you know what a signal means — ask. Direct communication is the best way to resolve a disagreement and restore connection.

Here's *my* rule: if you think you're disconnected, you are. If you feel like you're disconnected, you are. There is no such thing as a bad conversation about the relationship if the relationship is important to both of you. Conversations are especially important if you have children. They are the ones hurt worst by affairs, separations, and divorce.

When we come to the table to have a conversation with our partner, we all arrive with a set of beliefs and intentions. Sometimes, especially if we're upset, we have the intention to prove ourselves right, to make our partner feel the hurt that we're feeling, to regain control we think we've lost, and to vent our anger. All of these emotions are normal and yet none of them are helpful.

I have found, from my own experience and that of my clients, that it helps to believe that for the relationship to work, each partner needs to fully be themselves and see to their own needs *first* — before taking care of the other person. This is the best kind of self-care. By looking out for ourselves first, we can be fully present for our partner.

My partner and I create time to have serious conversations that meet both of our schedules, in a place where we can talk face-to-face, one-on-one, without distractions. We agree to use the discussion or argument to learn about ourselves, learn about each other, make our relationship stronger, and create more trust and intimacy. We use "I feel" statements, we practice reflective listening, and we do our best not to interrupt. And you know what? We do this whether we're having "a talk" or not. We share and let each other in because we enjoy getting to know each other more deeply.

Hey, it has gotten ugly in our household, we're not faultless, but we do our best to use the skills we've learned through experience and from experts. A relationship without arguments is abnormal. A relationship with unresolved arguments is normal, but unfortunate. A relationship that builds a pattern of successfully resolving arguments benefits from increased connection, not to mention spectacular make-up sex!

So many clients share issues with me that they don't share with their partner. This is because they feel safer when parts of themselves are secret. However, you don't know how your partner will think, feel, or act, and you may owe it to yourself to find out. In the tough conversations you discover what your relationship is made of. In the long term, keeping secrets costs you a piece of your authentic self and the life-affirming intimacy of an honest relationship. To prevent affairs, to have an extraordinary relationship, and even to simply be at peace in your own skin, being every inch of yourself is a risk that at some point you will have to take.

chapter 23
LIFE'S NOT FAIR

I don't know why life isn't fair. I do know that getting stuck in the *why* of unfairness has never brought me any peace or comfort. Asking why life's not fair has only indulged my inner demons and perpetuated my suffering.

Life, God, and the Universe are totally unfathomable. We don't know how the world is supposed to be. We think we do, however, which is why the world seems unfair. It doesn't match our preconceived notions. Therefore, we're all better off having faith in the world and in our situations exactly as they are.

What about tragedies like 9/11, or famine in foreign countries? What about when a family loses a child to a drunk driver? What about when beauty is rewarded over character, or nepotism is favored over talent?

None of these things seem fair to me, from my perspective, in this reality. But I know that there's much more to the world than me and my perspective and that this reality is not the only one.

For years I looked over my shoulder and compared myself to other people — their lives, their triumphs, their victories, their struggles, their everything. People were always above me or below me. It was exhausting. And because I was often focusing on what I didn't have, how life was unfair, and on what wasn't working in my life, the Universe supplied me more of that. But the moment that I discovered my life's purpose — who I am, why I'm here, and what I'm about — that all diminished. In an instant, I became the hottest game in town. Everybody lined up beside me and my whole life became crystal clear. I have learned that whatever I focus on expands. I now choose to focus on all that is amazing — me, my faith, my family, and on all that is working for me in my life. What a magnificent way to live.

Instead of lamenting the unfairness of life, be more fair to yourself. Reward yourself for jobs well done. Acknowledge your skills, abilities, and values. Count your blessings. Make a contribution to a cause you think is just. Enjoy the beauty in your world. Respond to what feels unfair by focusing on what is good.

chapter 24
The VALUE of LOSS, The DANGER of HAPPINESS

The greatest fallacy that we project is that we're going to live forever. Following that is the belief that life is "good" and death is "bad." Life and death, beginnings and endings, gain and loss are simply aspects of the same thing. You can't cherish one without the other — you also can't avoid one without avoiding the other.

Awareness of the necessity and the usefulness of death opens a door for passion to fill your life. This is why people who have a near-death experience and those who are nearing the end of their days often discover their truth. The nearness of death creates clarity beyond belief.

This awareness doesn't have to come from the threat of our own physical death. Death surrounds us all the time in the form of evolution. Plants and animals and species die so that other forms of life can live. Objects die or are discontinued — like the Betamax or eight-tracks or the Gremlin. But without those deaths we wouldn't have VHS or CDs or the Ford Explorer. Ideas die, like monarchy and slavery, and new ideas take their place, like democracy and freedom.

Let's not forget that a life change is a death of our self, not just a shedding of skin but the death of an old way of being and the birth of a new one. As we make ourselves anew, certain relationships pass on, making space for new friends, often better suited to who we are and not who we used to be.

This is the value of loss. Loss makes space for growth.

The danger of happiness is that many of us see being happy as a distraction from how we often feel. Our minds begin to ask, how can I hang onto this feeling? This is a recipe for misery if there ever was one, sort of like waking up on a beautiful day and insisting, from that day forth, that if it's not seventy-three and sunny that the weather is terrible. If your life is only on track when it's seventy-three and sunny, you'll be bitterly disappointed on most days. You won't appreciate the rain, snow, or clouds.

Thus, most of us chase happiness in the same way we might use a drug, hoping to make the pain go away — and it never does, does it? That's because you can't hide in happiness. It's not a place you get to; it's not a resort or a destination. It's just an emotion, the same as sadness or jealousy or confusion.

Plus, if we escape to Club Happiness to avoid dealing with painful feelings, those feelings need to become more painful in order to be heard. The result is that on top of chasing happiness we turn to distractions like shopping, drinking, sex, or drugs.

Loss, failure, setbacks — any of these is challenging. But when we feel worthless or doomed or hopeless or powerless *because* of our loss, we now face a greater challenge: suffering. Suffering is refusing to accept the reality of the loss, maintaining the fiction that the loss shouldn't have happened, didn't really happen, or isn't as hurtful as it feels. We feel bad, which, because we believe we're not supposed to feel bad, makes us feel worse.

Suffering impedes our journey. It is impossible to move through loss and learn its lessons without first dealing with the suffering that surrounds it. In a sense, if a life problem is like a bad toothache, and if loss is pulling the tooth, then suffering is stopping in mid-extraction.

Almost all of us unconsciously choose to suffer at some point in our lives. We thrive on being a victim. We need a new vehicle for our own drama. We feed on our pain and misery. Eventually, however, we refuse to tolerate living life in the middle of a dental operation. We acknowledge the loss and allow the suffering to dissipate.

Then we go back to basics. We notice our world; we feel our feelings, all of them. We sit with anger, fear, sadness, despair, destructiveness, guilt, disappointment, frustration, grief, hurt, and we ask: What is the lesson for me to learn in this opportunity that I've created for myself? We remind ourselves that we've made it through other tough times, that this will pass, and that we're bigger than our thoughts and feelings. We ask for help, we seek experts. And when the pain cuts too deeply, we drop to our knees and pray.

Prayer tends to be something that we do in moments of desperation. In the trenches during an air raid. Wiping vomit from our lips as we crouch over the toilet, purging. Crying hysterically in the shower after the death of a loved one. On our own deathbeds.

However, prayer is a powerful tool to integrate any kind of loss. We can pray for guidance when an adventure begins. We can ask for assistance when we reach a situation we think we can't handle ourselves. We can express gratitude for our victories along the way. In other words, we don't need to be forced to our knees to pray. We can choose to drop to our knees at any time.

chapter 25
The GAY PRIDE PARADE

We end prejudice not only by fighting for our rights, but by acting as if we already have them. The genius of Martin Luther King and Gandhi, to me, is not just that they fought peacefully and non-violently, but that they acted with such dignity that it became impossible for the ruling power to deny them their humanity.

This is a crucial and exciting moment in gay history. Gay marriage is becoming a mainstream issue and there are more openly gay people than ever. The battle has begun in this country to define freedom once again.

The time has come for everyone who is gay to take a searching moral inventory of themselves. Which lessons, what wisdom, what legacy are you leaving to the next generation of gay Americans? Getting publicly wrecked during a gay pride event doesn't inspire pride

— it perpetuates homophobia. Why should gay culture be expressed through excess and overindulgence? Gay pride events are a chance to showcase the best of our culture: creativity, boldness, charisma, artistry — but also compassion, fun, and love — and especially integrity, honor, and fairness.

We must speak with one voice, and that means ending the petty divisions in our own backyard. Transsexuals, transgenders, and bisexuals are human beings, just like you and me. Let's unite. We can use all of the love and support that we can get, especially from our own community.

Despite sexual and racial equality laws, sexism and racism still exist in this country. It would be naïve to think that homophobia will vanish any faster than, say, anti-Semitism. However, just because it is a long battle doesn't mean it isn't worth fighting. Every gay American has a chance to take a stand on behalf of the human race, right now. Be yourself, live with dignity, and let others see that diversity is an asset, that equality is a right, and that we are all united by a common humanity.

chapter 26
GOOD JUDGMENT
Comes from BAD JUDGMENT

When you think about the vast number of actions we take in a day, we rarely, if ever, choose to act. Most actions arise spontaneously from the nature of the self. Many decisions that you believe were carefully considered may have been nothing more than psychological reflexes. For example, did you choose who to date? Or did the chemistry when your eyes met make the decision for you? How about what to order off a menu? Did you "choose," or did your past experiences in that restaurant, combined with your particular tastes, your hunger at that time of day, and the smells wafting through the restaurant "choose" for you? You probably

knew (unconsciously) what you were going to have before you even sat down.

If the actions we take are often pre-determined by
circumstances, other people, our own conditioning, and
by basic laws of nature, it would seem as though we're
completely out of control almost all of the time. Our social, economic, and political worlds are in constant upheaval. Our behavior is profoundly influenced by our
environment. Our minds, trained through experience,
respond in predictable stimulus-response patterns.
Therefore, at the same time that we live in a chaotic
world full of interdependent forces, our egos strive to
maintain order and consistency.

One way we do this is to maintain the illusion that
we have choice when we do not. To choose is a very specific and powerful act that requires complete presence
in the moment, dissolution of the past, and detachment
from outcomes. In short, choosing is an act of someone
who knows at the deepest level that this moment is all
there is, that the past doesn't exist and doesn't need to
influence the present, and that the future doesn't exist
and therefore neither do potential outcomes. A choice
is the act of a highly conscious being.

This idea can seem scary because of the comfort we
derive from the illusion of choice. If we have choice, we

think, then we're in control of our world. Then we're safe. However, if there is any safety in the world, it's not in the illusion of control. It's in our commitment to acknowledge our present reality and learn despite our unconsciousness.

A choice most of us can make is to learn. Learning is the great game of life. Our instincts and all the other factors out of our control take us into situations. We take responsibility for our actions and absorb the consequences of those situations. Our instincts, as a result, get better.

Eventually you have what is known as good judgment. How did that happen? Lots of bad judgment. You stand on your failures, not your successes. Choices, true acts of free will, are made by people who trust, risk, fail, and learn.

chapter 27
Let Yourself OFF THE HOOK

It's 10:00 P.M. Jack's seeking refuge in a bottle of Crown Royal at a nearby bar while Jill's curled up on the living room couch with a quart of vanilla chip. Jack and Jill both work, have been married nine years, and have recently filed for divorce. Their relationship abounds with difficult issues, none of which compare to the troubles they're passing along to their eight-year-old son, Joe, who spends each day tormented by stomach pains, headaches, anxiety, and feelings he doesn't understand.

Jack, Jill, and Joe all feel the same dominant emotion. They all feel GUILT. Please pause for a moment and consider how strangely accurate it is for all of them, in their different circumstances, with different problems and different backgrounds, to all feel the same emotion.

Why does Jack feel guilty?

- It could be because he initiated the divorce proceedings — and as a result, Jill was hurt very deeply. Of course, he's not responsible for her feelings. She could have just as easily let out a sigh of relief and said thank you.
- Jack could feel guilty because he's not being a good father to Joe. Of course, he doesn't really know that. Perhaps long-term exposure to his alcoholism would be much worse for Joe, and while the divorce is unfortunate, it's the better alternative.
- Jack could feel guilty because he's destroying his liver and shortening his life span and risking getting fired from his job. He wants to be a good father, a good provider, a good husband, but his life situation isn't ideal and he's doing the best he knows how.

We can each look back on our lives and see times where we did insane, destructive things that were absolutely necessary. We stand on our failures, not on our successes. Sometimes, an "error" is the seed of a lesson we can use down the road. This is part of what's so mysterious about the ways of the Universe and God's grand design. It's just not possible to look at a man drinking and say that he's not supposed to be doing that. We're better off assuming that drinking is exactly what he's supposed to be doing at this moment. We're better off having faith and feeling some compassion for Jack, and for that matter, so is Jack — Jack could have faith and trust in his situation, as bleak as it may seem. Having an alcohol problem and the inner demons that go with it is troubling enough. Jack could have some compassion for himself. But he doesn't. He feels guilty.

Meanwhile, Jill is coping with the demands of a full-time job on top of the cooking and cleaning and carpool that goes along with motherhood. Her life is especially tough because Joe is frequently sick and sometimes will beg or throw tantrums to get whatever he wants. She's so tired and so busy that she gives in, hoping it will appease him, but only making him into more of a tyrant. On top of this, her husband has asked her for a divorce and is slowly drinking himself into oblivion. Her world is falling apart and the ice cream that gives her a moment's peace every day has added thirty pounds and four inches to her waist.

Why does Jill feel guilty?

- Perhaps it's because she thinks her weight gain drove her husband to drink and ask for the divorce. Then again, she's not responsible for his actions; he could just as easily have asked her if she'd go to relationship counseling. Besides, a divorce might be preferable to raising her son alongside a father with an alcohol problem.

- Maybe she feels guilty because she thinks she's not being a good mom, although if she could view her situation from a distance she'd see that a full-time job, a compulsive overeating problem, and the demands of a second-grade sultan would be too much for anyone. That she's managed to survive this long is an achievement in itself.

Now, Joe, poor Joe, Joe's just a kid. As children we believe that our world is all about us — we're supposed to, that's the nature of children. Sure, Joe acts out, doesn't clean his room, and complains about feeling sick a lot of the time, but he's eight for God's sake and reacting to the rift in his parent's marriage. He feels guilty because he thinks the rift is his fault and the divorce will be, too. What do we expect, for him to politely request family therapy?

Let's return to Jack and Jill. Jack thinks that the destruction of his family wouldn't be happening if he was the perfect man, the perfect husband, and the perfect father that he's supposed to be — the kind of man who shrugs off the abuse he received at the hands of his own alcoholic father, parents a well-behaved child, and maintains a great marriage. He feels guilty for the same reason Joe does: he doesn't know how to accept his reality. The reality is that he survived abuse, the reality is that he has a genetic heritage that predisposes him to alcoholism, the reality is that he and his wife need help and he doesn't know how to ask for it. Still, he needs the fantasy that he's in perfect control of his world and that it's possible for him to fix everything.

Jill also feels responsible for everything because she also maintains the fiction that she's in control. She wouldn't gain weight, Joe wouldn't misbehave, and Jack wouldn't drink if she was the perfect wife — the woman who, despite her own unresolved guilt over her own parents' divorce, knows just how to help her husband, flawlessly raise her child, cook and clean like Martha Stewart, and effortlessly stay a size six. She feels guilty for the same reasons Jack and Joe do: she doesn't know how to accept the reality that she's not perfect.

Guilt is an emotion we feel when we think we're supposed to be someone we're not — someone in control of uncontrollable things, someone perfect. Guilt is a symptom of the disease of perfectionism and of the illusion we maintain that we're in control over everything in our lives. Guilt is insane. How can we be anyone other than who we are? Why take a difficult situation, like a drinking problem or a compulsive eating disorder, and make it worse by feeling guilty about it? We might as well make it even worse by punishing ourselves for feeling inappropriately guilty about our difficult situation.

The illusion of control, the illusion of perfection, is a whip you use to lash yourself because you think that if you hurt enough you'll make the right changes in order to create the outcomes you desire. In fact, the opposite is true. It is by accepting yourself that desires manifest.

What would you be feeling if you weren't feeling guilty? It's a good bet that you'd feel sadness or grief or anger or some other uncomfortable emotion. The fiction of perfection and control and the guilt that accompanies it can be a way to hide from underlying emotions. However, it is experiencing, processing, and being with these subterranean feelings that is the healing path.

So let yourself off the hook. You're doing the best you can. Practice acceptance, and you will find yourself acting in your best interests, not protecting a fantasy of perfection.

chapter 28
SHARE a MOMENT

One of the most difficult times in your life will be when a close friend or family member gets very sick. I'm sorry to say it, but you can count on this happening. The silver lining is that with every crisis comes opportunity, and when a loved one is ill, it's a chance to share a moment with them that can deepen and strengthen your relationship forever.

Many of us find out that a friend is sick and have a hard time getting to the hospital to visit them. We have a hard time picking up the phone. It's partly because we're not sure what to say, but mostly because their mortality awakens us to our own. Their crisis triggers ours.

Suddenly this becomes not only an opportunity to strengthen the relationship but to learn something about ourselves. What does this friend or relative contribute to you that you are no longer receiving? Is there anything you need to say or communicate, any unfinished business? Does the thought of losing them activate unresolved grief from a loss of your own? Most importantly, who can you count on to support you so that you can better support your friend?

This last question is vital. Don't expect that you'll be able to grit your teeth and just "handle it." You need to be available for someone else and you can't do that if you've got too much on your own plate. This is not an appropriate time for the relationship to be about you. Please be present with all of your feelings, but make arrangements with other friends or a counselor to act as a support network. Even though this is more difficult for your loved one, it's hard for you, too.

First, you have to show up.

Then, listen. Listening is the key that unlocks the door to those tingling moments of connection and intimacy. Platitudes like "You'll be fine" or "You'll get through this" or "This will only make you stronger" can invalidate and dismiss the experience of the person who is ill. It seems as though we say these things for their benefit, but it's usually to make ourselves feel better.

What soothes both you and your loved one is the intimate connection of your authentic selves. A very ill person is undergoing a profound change, a radical shifting of priorities, and frequently the mundane concerns of daily living have vanished. Listening allows you to embrace the person they are in this moment and provides for the magical transformation of loneliness, alienation, and fear into support, connection, and faith.

I've never had the honor of bringing a child into this world or seeing a child brought into this world, but I have had the honor and privilege of being with one of my best friends as he returned home. That night I held one of his hands and his lover of eighteen years held the other; both of us present to nurture, calm, and soothe him as he gasped for breath. It was excruciating to watch him struggle, yet I also felt an overwhelming sense of peace knowing that he was going to be okay as he ventured home. There would be no more suffering for him. I am grateful that this courageous man let me be there with him through his transition.

When we're older and looking back on our lives, our memories will be imperfect. We will have had so many experiences — so many dates, meals, injuries, successes, failures, parking tickets, and laughs — that it will be impossible to remember them all. However, these moments, these powerful moments of authentic connection with someone you love, will nourish and sustain you and live in your heart forever.

chapter 29
The RIPENING

Age is not a limitation; it's an opportunity to contribute more and more. At any age, it is possible to improve ourselves, to live a fuller, richer life, and to realize the essential nature of our humanity: a life of meaningful contribution to yourself and others.

Ripening is a word that implies improvement with age, and I believe that ripening isn't just for fruits and vegetables. People, too, have the potential to get better with age — to become more at peace, more in tune, more grounded, more fulfilled, more conscious. I want to be physically healthy for as long as possible, so I take great care of myself. I believe in drinking lots of pure water, avoiding caffeine and other drugs, and wearing sunscreen. Also on behalf of my physical body, I do my best to live in balance, make time for rest and play, strengthen my connection to God, and give and receive love.

Still, no matter how good a life we lead, no matter how much care we take with our diet and exercise programs, one day there will be gray hair and more. Our physical health and vitality deteriorate as we get older. The truth of aging, however, is that while we age physically, we can ripen emotionally and spiritually. Every one of us has this potential.

My experience with cancer illuminated this for me. At that time I had little control over my physical body, but I ripened emotionally and spiritually. While I was going through my cancer surgery and treatments, so many friends and family sent cards, e-mails, cookies, bears, flowers, prayers, and even put me in prayer chains. I had always conceptually understood that people loved me, but because of this experience I could genuinely *feel* how much people loved me. The generosity of others expanded my ability to receive, and my heart was cracked wide open.

I remember walking down the halls of the oncology ward at Cedars-Sinai Hospital and my mother, clearly upset, distraught, and devastated, yet trying to keep her cool for me, asked, "Why do you think that this is happening to you?" Without missing a beat, I said,

"Mom, I know exactly why this is happening. God is opening up my heart so that I can make room for the love of my life to come in." See, up until that point, I never genuinely felt loveable. I felt love, but not loveable. I would open my heart and then shut it. Then I'd open it up a bit more and then shut it again. Cancer, love, generosity and my own faith and openness ripened me. I now welcome the years.

If we do our best to live in the moment, to give ourselves work we enjoy, to surround ourselves with people we love and who love us, to strengthen our "why to live" each passing day, then aging can be a time of joyous harvesting. Bitter experiences from the past, with enough time, effort, and surrender, mature into sweetness. The challenge and the opportunity of this ripening is to share this sweetness with others — and to sip a little ourselves.

chapter 30
Go BEHIND the CURTAIN

There are those who benefit greatly from participating in organized religion. However, my experience is that most people are so desperate to know the nature of the world and their place in it that they are willing to adopt views that often limit them — views that are detached from their authenticity and that deny them their authenticity. For so many, an organized religion is a community of people who have agreed to imprison themselves individually in order to have membership in the group.

Have you ever had someone try to convert you? It's as if they think that if they can get you to agree with them and think what they think, it will help convince them that they aren't abandoning themselves in favor of the tenets of their religion. People who try to function as missionaries aren't necessarily trying to save your soul — they may be trying to get you to save theirs.

Guilt is one of the great motivators and protectors of humanity. When parents teach their children right from wrong, they are relying on a built-in guilt mechanism that helps the child remember. The idea is that when we do "right," we feel good, and when we do "wrong," we feel bad. This works until we reach an age where we recognize that good and bad and right and wrong are relative, subjective, and often very complicated. After this realization we use our common sense to make decisions instead of just doing what we've always been told to do.

Religion can be a guilt amplifier. It can magnify guilt to such an extent that it can provoke violence. Consider how many religions teach love, forgiveness, and non-violence, and consider how many lives have been lost because of wars fought over who worships the right god. There is an obvious contradiction here.

Here's how it works: religion is a set of rules about what you're supposed to do and not do but also about what you're supposed to think and not think. When you do and think the right things you go to "heaven," and when you don't you go to "hell." Now, when you are with a group of people all dressed relatively the same, and you all stand and sit at the same time, speak and sing the same words, agree to do and think the same things, this creates a sense of community and belonging.

However, this is a false sense of security. When you create insiders, you create outsiders. Insiders, the people who stand and sit and speak and think and do just as you do, are seen as good and worthy. Outsiders are often seen as bad and unworthy. This is why Christians of many denominations tolerate racism in their ranks. This is why many secular Muslims tolerate the fanatics who blow up innocent civilians. Whether due to race, religion, or gender, when you create and value insiders it becomes easy to hate and demonize outsiders — this is why the Holocaust happened, why all ethnic cleansing happens. Religion is a force that makes it possible to see the human being who agrees with you as a neighbor, and the one who doesn't as an animal or an enemy or a piece of trash.

Are there good Christians, good Jews, good Muslims, good religious people sourced in faith and compassion? Absolutely. There are also very compassionate and wise members of all-white country clubs. There are merciful and well-intentioned heroin dealers. Just because you're a good person who finds comfort in religion doesn't make religion necessarily a good thing.

Religion, for many, can be an obstacle to true connection to God. For example, all religions have prefabricated prayers. These prayers were chosen a long time ago in a very different era for human culture and society. Two thousand years later, it's kind of like sending mass-produced junk mail to God.

Prayer isn't just the words you say, it's the sentiment in your heart when you say it. It is an intensely personal form of expression. A real prayer is like a real letter — not a form letter, but something written in the present moment in your own words.

I believe in God and my faith is strong. I believe in a loving God that accepts all of who I am without reservation or limits. I am grateful for my connection to God for I know that he lives inside of me (and inside of each and every one of us). It has never been him that hasn't loved me or accepted me during any part in my journey, it's always been him creating opportunities for me to deepen my level of love and acceptance for myself. His love is pure and fills my light with infinite radiance.

The truth is that faith is different from religion. Faith is knowing that God lives within you as well as without and that your relationship is unique and personal. Religion instructs everyone (for the most part) to have the same beliefs and to follow the same sets of behaviors. Faith reflects the reality that we are individuals first and members of groups second. Religion can treat you as a marketing representative for its agenda and can also tell you which side of an opposition you're supposed to be on. Your faith, on the other hand, can awaken compassion and humanity and inspire the desire for peace.

chapter 31
COME OUT of the CLOSET

If you've had an abortion, that doesn't define you. Neither does jail time. Neither does profound self-loathing, staying in an abusive relationship, or being barren. Maybe you always lie about your age or your weight or the fact that you got kicked out of college. Maybe you have a degenerative disease or a medical condition or an eating disorder. Maybe you're having a torrid affair. Maybe you're deep in credit card debt. Maybe you have an illegal drug problem — a legal drug problem — an over-the-counter drug problem, perhaps?

You have permission to be who you are, to keep parts of yourself safe and protected in the closet. That's what the closet's for; it gives us time to store up energy and courage. Sometimes we need to wait for the moment when we can take that big leap of faith and believe that we are perfect just as we are, that we are worthy of life and love, worthy of a place in this world, worthy of being seen and heard and accepted. The closet is there for a reason and you should use it if you need to — I have, we all have. But there is a danger if you keep yourself hidden for too long — like a plant that's not getting enough sunlight, if you don't come out of the closet, your authentic self can shrivel and die.

We keep parts of ourselves in the closet because we think we will gain acceptance and validation from others. We want certain people in our lives, often friends we've had for a long time and family we can't imagine doing without. However, the price of concealing ourselves is intimacy — the people who accept and validate us don't know who we truly are. We feel alone and alienated. Slowly, the pressure builds, until suddenly those secret self-parts trapped in the closet start trying to get out, like Poe's tell-tale heart, thumping and beating and screaming for attention. Coming out doesn't happen all at once. I will forever be coming out, because coming out, for me, means deepening my level of honesty with and within myself, for myself, and about myself. I am grateful that I will always be dropping deeper and deeper into my truth. For me, that is freedom.

In fact, coming out is an evolution with different stages of acceptance. At each stage, you swing the closet door open, take a deep breath, and say, "Here I am." Remember, you are a human being. You can forgive yourself for not being perfect. You are bigger than your secrets. And when you take a stand for yourself, you pave the way for others to do the same.

It's okay to open the door slowly. It's okay to peek your head out, look around, and go back inside where it's safe. Kick the door down if you want to, but for most of us it's baby steps, baby steps to come out of the closet. The important thing is to honor your pace, and here's what you need to do first: build a safe haven. Reveal yourself to people who you believe will welcome you. If you don't know anyone like that, find a life coach or a support group or a therapist or all three. Be as kind to yourself as possible.

There will be people who go into the closet as you come out. There will be those who love and admire you for who you are, and there will be those who can't. Honor your own timing. Trust your instincts. You may want to reveal yourself to one person at a time, you may want to tell a room of fifty. Your journey is your own, so only you determine what pace feels comfortable. Remember that when you reveal yourself to someone you are giving them a magnificent gift. It is a privilege to receive you, to see you stand with courage in an intimate, vulnerable moment. While *you* know that, everyone will receive you in their own way. You need to allow them to have that experience. Some relationships will deepen. Some will change. Some may fade away. This is the risk you take when you understand that living your authentic life is worth it.

Once we step up to the plate and begin the process of coming out, it's natural for our social world to get mixed up a bit and to settle down in a different form. We can't prevent our world from changing, but we can participate in the communities and groups and relationships that recognize and appreciate us for who we are. We can harness the power of our secrets for connection and intimacy. When we are willing to simply be ourselves, relationships become more loving and more nurturing, and there is ample fuel inside us for living life to the fullest.

chapter 32
Learn "WHY" to Learn "HOW"

What is a good life? We may fantasize that it involves success, a perfect family, a perfect relationship, fame and fortune, but we know that there is no such thing as perfection and that frequently "success" takes a problem and makes it worse. Equating a good life with our fantasy is an easy way to feel bad. All we have to do is look around, watch TV, see all the rich good-looking happy people, and think to ourselves, *Life's unfair. It never works out for me. I'm just going to stay on autopilot, keep my head down, lock my true feelings inside. I'll find comfort in a bottle, a shoe store, a casino, or an éclair.*

So let's not do that, okay? What is a good life? For most of us, the answer is that we simply don't know. Life is the journey into the unknown to find that out. You see, you can have the life of your dreams if you're willing to acknowledge that you may not know what that is — and yet be willing to handle your considerations anyway.

Considerations are issues, problems, annoyances, things like the rent or the mortgage, getting the kids to school, taking the car in for service, paying your bills, feeling like you never have enough time. Considerations are also the daily battles with nagging relatives, annoying people at the office, troublesome clients, even those awful inner voices telling you that you're not good enough. Considerations are the struggles to enjoy the body you have, to eat in moderation, to appreciate your partner, to love yourself despite your (perceived) flaws. Considerations are especially fears and anxieties of loss and failure, as well as fears of success and greatness, and most especially, fear of the unknown.

You will always have them. Considerations will always be there. If you handle one, another will surface. The question is, can you enjoy learning from the ones you've got? Remember, everything is happening FOR you, not TO you. The goal is not to eliminate your considerations so you can live in peace, the goal is to live in peace with your considerations. They are as much a part of your life as your friends or your home or your body.

You can live authentically, when you want to. You can handle your considerations when you have good enough reasons. So....why DO you get out of bed in the morning?

If you don't know, that's okay. Searching for meaning in your life can be as fun and joyful as finding it. Confusion, despair, stress, and strain can be your friends and teachers. The lessons they bring are golden.

One of the great lessons is the importance of balance. Many of us have a fantasy of balance, usually a carefree life of ease with few considerations. Real balance is not a state of perfection, real balance is a process of adjusting. Ever see a man walk the tightrope? He doesn't stroll comfortably. He stays alert. He shifts his weight, his hands, his feet. Though he sways and falters, slowly he makes his way across. He does whatever it takes to keep his feet on the rope. That's balance.

The key to balance is establishing the priorities of — you guessed it — your considerations. You may be wondering how this is done, but the question is not HOW, the question is WHY. Why do you need to establish priorities? Why is it important to stay in balance? Why is it worth it for you to handle your considerations?

For me, I have a job that connects me intimately with several people every day. I care about my clients. I use my skills to help them look beautiful on the outside and I use my life experience to help them feel their authentic beauty on the inside. I love my work and I am valuable to my clients — however, being a hairapist can be quite challenging. It takes a lot of time and energy and mental and emotional resources.

Therefore, in order to take care of my clients, I must take care of myself first. Time at the gym is non-negotiable. It's my early morning meditation time and I give myself that so that I can truly and unconditionally give myself to others. Nutritious food is non-negotiable. So is date night. So is prayer.

If I am feeling overwhelmed, I do the best I can to keep my feet on the rope. I prioritize, I renegotiate, I delegate, I meditate, and I ask for help. I trust that what's happening is happening FOR me, not TO me. I ask for my lessons, I surrender to what is, I feel my feelings, and if I fall off the rope... you guessed it — I take a deep breath and I get right back on.

Think about the relationship between considerations (which you will always have), balance (which is essential to handling considerations), and life management skills (what you use to create balance) as a triangle. At the center of the triangle is a big question: WHY? Why do you live? Why do you get up in the morning?

Victor Frankl found an answer during the Second World War. He was a Jewish psychologist who spent years researching and writing a book on the importance of finding meaning in life. Before he could publish it, the Nazis stripped him of his property, his family, and his possessions, but he managed to hide the manuscript in his coat. When he got to Auschwitz he was literally stripped of his clothing, losing his manuscript, and forced to wear the rags of a prisoner who had been sent to the gas chamber. Inside the pocket of one of the rags was a page from the Bible. Frankl determined that this was a sign from God and decided that he needed to live, that as a psychologist he had the ability to learn from the horror and bring something useful back to the world. He was not young or strong or tough, but he had a reason to stay alive, and while many younger and stronger and tougher men died, he survived. After Auschwitz was liberated he wrote a book called *Man's Search for Meaning*, and in it he writes a phrase from Nietzsche I hope will resonate within you. Remember this when life gets tough: "He who has a 'why' to live can bear almost any 'how'."

chapter 33
PERCOLATE

Almost every time you learn something valuable, that learning is preceded by a time when you were stuck. Celebrate "stuckness." It means something extraordinary is coming.

However, it might not be what you think. Sometimes a trial or a period of adversity results in becoming stronger. Sometimes it doesn't — but who's to say that stronger is always better? In a powerful wind, the oak tree will break. The bamboo, weaker than the oak, will surrender to the wind, be blown about, and survive. We live in a culture of yang, of strength, of action, of progress; but there is value in yin, weakness, stillness, and silence.

Stuckness is the feeling of not learning a lesson. In reality, you are learning, just not at the conscious level.

Consciously, it seems like you continue to be given the same lesson over and over again. We date the same kinds of people, face the same kinds of issues, have many of the same conversations over and over and over again until we're sick of the words coming out of our mouths. What's really happening is that, slowly, the tectonic plates of our psychology are shifting. Stuckness is a state of preparation. Once we're ready to pursue a new path, the path reveals itself.

If we can agree that feeling stuck is an inevitable part of life, the question becomes how to *be* with it. I call this process "percolating." There's a kind of coffeemaker that allows the water to drip through the grinds, then shoots the coffee back up to drip through the grinds again, and again, until the coffee is rich and powerful.

That's what I do when I'm stuck, or rather I should say, when I *feel* stuck. I sit with the problem or issue and allow it to drench me over and over until the information and the experience absorb and re-absorb into different levels of my being, until I've got it deeply enough that I learn something. Sometimes, I have an insight. Sometimes, my perspective on a relationship or an issue changes completely. This is the gift of stuckness — the opportunity to learn something new.

PERCOLATE

Self-help books are a way of percolating because almost all self-help books, tapes, and programs are trying to teach the same things. Some of the books that have inspired me are *The Power of Now, The Four Agreements, You Can Heal Your Life, I Had It All the Time, Anatomy of the Spirit,* and *The Artist's Way.* These books are like paths, and no matter which path you take, they all lead to the same place — a place of truth, peace, acceptance, and faith. It's your journey that is unique. If you don't get what you want out of a self-help book, if you don't begin to move through your pain or receive the guidance you need, try another. Percolate.

chapter 34
AND

Life is growth, not maintenance. The only way you can preserve who you are is to climb into a vat of embalming fluid and drown yourself. In life, we grow and change.

And is about realizing that we are best able to grow when we know that we are bigger than our titles, images, and labels. They can kill our spirits if we try to inhabit them, but they can enhance who we are if we can put them on and take them off like clothes. We wear what's appropriate for the occasion and we never confuse who we are with what we're wearing or what's hanging in our closet.

At different times… I am a hairstylist. And a life coach. And a spouse. And a son. And a friend. And an athlete. I am brave and thoughtful and timid and scared. I am smart, creative, mundane, dense, and spectacular. I feel exhausted and balanced and energized and frenzied and hopeful and frustrated and peaceful. And I doubt. And I wonder. And so much more.

Simply put, you and I have the capacity to feel and experience everything. What stops us is the sense that our identities will only be preserved if we maintain narrow definitions of ourselves. We feel an emotion we don't want, like anger, and we stifle it, saying to ourselves, "I'm not an angry person. Sure, I get frustrated, but I'm not angry." Well, surprise! Sometimes, you're angry! Sometimes, you're really pissed! If you don't experience anger you are like a teapot that is boiling and never gets to let off any steam — the heat's there, the pressure's there — you've just got the lid on too tightly! Which means... no whistling... no alert to turn the gas off... no tea... and eventually, an explosion.

Thank God that I learned to put an *and* in my life and to take out the *or*. That *and* saved my life. For years I was trying to prove to myself that I wasn't selfish, so I would abandon myself at all costs to do whatever was needed of me to do, to prove to me that I wasn't selfish. For me, I was always either generous or selfish. When I gave myself the permission to be selfish *and* selfless, my whole world opened up. I learned that neither one carries more weight than the other. It's okay for me to be both. My ego no longer defines me.

Your ego is a description of who you are, not the truth of who you are. Your ego is like a biography combined with an extensive resume and a huge picture album. That's not your authentic self. Who you are is only who you are being right now, in this moment, and that is something that cannot be labeled or described on a piece of paper.

Your name is not who you are. Your name is a series of sounds that you agree to respond to. Your name is a series of letters that you agree to sign when you want to be legally bound to something. Remember when Prince tried to get out of this trap of labels and images by changing his name to a symbol? Didn't work — he became "the Artist formerly known as Prince," and if you wanted to buy one of his albums, you went into the record store and looked under "Prince." This is how intensely our society requires us to separate and sort the world, to make tiny little categories and subcategories of objects and people and feelings and, well, everything.

Take a look around the room you are in. Your eyes naturally separate objects from each other. You can tell that the door is different from the wall and that the magazine lying on the table is not part of the table. It's natural and useful to be able to distinguish and categorize, otherwise you wouldn't be able to use the door to exit the room.

.   It's also natural to apply that same urge to categorize to yourself, but remember, who you are will expand and contract and change from moment to moment. So when you notice yourself, don't define yourself. Don't carve your image in stone. Don't take a snapshot of who you are and try to inhabit it. Just be who you are in this moment. And be who you are in the next moment. And the next. You'll change. That's how you know you're alive.

chapter 35
ADVANCED MATERIAL
(Use at Your Own Risk)

Doing, ceaseless doing, is how most of us live our lives. We feel this yawning emotional chasm within and we try to fill it with external validation, with success. We try to get others to love us enough to make that inner pain go away, and when that doesn't work we go to plan B: distractions, avoidances, and suffering. Part of what I'm hoping to communicate to you is that the inner pain ceases to be so destructive when you learn to be a human being, not a human doing. So much of this book is about the importance of being, of being in the moment, being with your feelings, being with another person, being with yourself.

Being requires faith, acceptance, and trust. Being is

simple, but not easy. This is because from the moment we are born we are thrust into a world of doing. Yes, as kids we play and make up games, and that's a form of being. But we also watch adults doing things all day long, and soon we long to grow up and we also must learn how to do things. We must learn how to read and write, walk the dog, put on make-up, do the dishes, take exams. The older we get, the more important doing becomes.

Especially in the fast-paced world of the information age, there are more things to do than ever. Families need two and three jobs to have enough income to have a chance to send their kids to college, or, God willing, take a much-needed vacation. Children need to learn to do so much more to acquire the skills to be competitive in the job market. The United States is the wealthiest country in the world in terms of money, but many of us are emotionally and spiritually impoverished.

We live in the world we choose to live in. You live in a world of your own making, and I live in a world of my own making. You wouldn't have your life if you didn't need it to be exactly the way it is in order for you to learn the lessons you need on this part of your journey. This idea, that we choose our world, implies some control over our circumstances. That stands to reason.

After all, if we learn some new skills, we can get a better job and make more money. If we get on an Internet dating service and start putting ourselves out there, we may meet wonderful new people. If we eat healthier and exercise more, we can transform our bodies.

And yet, one of the most critical and most difficult spiritual lessons is acceptance. Acceptance is when you acknowledge reality, whether you like it or not — and your like or dislike is part of what you accept! It can be difficult to practice acceptance because there is so much in the world that challenges our reality. Can we accept discomfort, confusion, and loneliness? Can we accept the obesity and poverty and homophobia in our nation? Can we accept war around the globe, bullies on the playground, and how much we pay for gasoline these days? Can we accept our fears of the unknown, our grief at losing loved ones, our anger, our frustration? Can we truly accept our successes, our magnificence as human beings, our divine nature?

Now we come to the paradox: we live in a world of our own making and that gives us choices for how to change it. In order to change our situation and improve our lives, we must first accept ourselves. In order to improve our world, we must accept our world. But when I say that I want to be different than I am, doesn't that mean that I don't accept myself? And if life is about the journey, not the destination, why do I desire certain outcomes so much? And if I do have control over my life, if I do choose my world in certain ways, why can't I actually create certain outcomes?

Well, you can. It's just that it requires you to do a great deal of work internally first. For example, it would seem like losing weight should be so easy. After all, the doing is fairly well defined: eat better, exercise more. Sure, you can follow this diet or that diet, this trainer's program of sets and reps and cardio or that one, but let's be honest, the basic formula is eat better and move your body more. It shouldn't be so hard, but we all know it is. We need to learn to understand and accept our relationship with food, which requires us to feel our submerged feelings, meet our own emotional needs, and accept ourselves to the best of our abilities. At that point, whether or not we go back to the buffet becomes a meaningful spiritual question on a journey that requires every ounce of strength we've got.

Most of this book is about the importance of being. Writing about how to achieve goals only from the perspective of doing, to me, is like writing a book about diet and exercise that doesn't take into account the profound spiritual relationship each of us has with our sources of nourishment. And yet, writing a book about how to achieve goals only from the perspective of being, to me, is like writing a diet and exercise book that doesn't discuss any of the merits of food combination or the importance of the glycemic index or the danger of trans-fatty acids.

When you get that you have the power to change your world and when you also begin to accept your world, then change becomes possible. You learn how to "be inside of doing." For example, when I go to the gym, I am definitely involved in doing. I've got an agenda for my physical health, I've still got some pride locked up in my self-image, and I like being a part of the social world at the gym. However, when I'm exercising, I totally allow myself to be. All of my conscious goals are gone, background noise at best. I enjoy my process. I feel my body. I let myself swim in the music. And before I know it, the workout is over. The pleasure I take in simply being inside of the doing (of exercise) is what makes it so gratifying for me to go to the gym.

What many of us do, however, is pretend to accept our world because we want to change so badly that we're willing to do whatever it takes. Unfortunately we haven't really learned acceptance, we've just taken our own obsession and brought it into the world of spirituality.

In the gym example, we try to love our bodies and we try to meditate while we exercise, but many of us are primarily there to lose weight and look better so we can find Mr. Right and settle down, or to tone up so we can feel okay about ourselves. This is practicing extreme non-acceptance masquerading as acceptance, and it's an easy way to burn out at the gym or to create a life where you're constantly forcing yourself to do things you don't want to do. It is smothering your authentic self in false authenticity.

What follows is my method of achieving outcomes without risking burnout or requiring distractions. It is a synthesis of methods I've learned and used over the years, so, of course, it includes my own spin. I think the key is in the earlier part of this chapter. It's not enough to learn how to DO, and it's not enough to learn how to BE. You have to know both.

- *Identify*: This first stage is naming and labeling the outcome you want. Whether it's inner peace, a car, Mr. Right, a transformed body, a great job, or waking up in the morning rested and rejuvenated, identify the specific features that you desire. It is important to be as honest and as detailed as possible.

- *Express Gratitude*: Thank your Higher Power for granting you your wish. Act as if it is done and show your appreciation. It can feel a little strange when you first start to do it, but this is how one makes requests of the divine — you act as if you're already at the finish line. You say thank you.

- *Visualize*: See in your mind the outcome you desire. I like to make it a ritual by lighting candles, closing my eyes, and praying over my intention (from the Identify stage), but whatever your method, you must see yourself having the outcome you desire.

- *Feel*: Imagine you've achieved your goal. Feel those feelings. For example, what does it feel like to be able to fully receive your partner's love? What does it feel like to live in your dream home? What does it feel like to be with Mr. Right? What does it feel like to find the perfect buyer for your old motorcycle? This process works with everything, but you have to be willing to let yourself go enough to feel the having of something that doesn't yet exist as if it actually exists, and to believe it!

- *Let Go*: This requires trust — and can therefore be the most challenging part of the process. However, after you've declared it, visualized it, and felt it, you've got to let it go. Stop the obsessing. Ease up on the anxiety. Don't think about it, don't worry about it, just keep being and feeling your way through life and allow your dreams and desires to manifest. Letting go can be so tough because we started this process when we wanted something, and we still want it, and now we've declared it, visualized it, been feeling it… and it's not here yet! So… it's tempting to declare again and in a new way, visualize more, feel more deeply… and wash, rinse, repeat. However, letting go is what makes it possible for what you want to arrive. Once you truly believe it, it will be.

Top athletes understand this process intuitively. Take baseball, for example. When a batter steps up to the plate, he inwardly declares his intentions, perhaps to get on base, perhaps to hit a fly ball and bring home a runner. He visualizes making contact; he visualizes where he wants the ball to go. Because of his previous experience, he has an easy time imagining and feeling that solid connection that results in a hit, and he takes a few practice swings before the pitcher winds up. Then, as the pitcher releases, he stops thinking and lets go — he surrenders and swings. He lets his body figure it out.

That's how this process works. Identify. Ask. Surrender. We use our conscious minds to assist us, lovingly, to help us identify and ask for what we want. Then we surrender and allow our unconscious minds to manifest it for us.

chapter 36
The BOUNDARIES of LOVE

Boundaries are necessary for growth. Without bark, a tree will die. Without the membrane, there is no cell. Even the growth of the United States of America can be attributed to the Pacific and Atlantic oceans, which act as a natural boundary. Humans have sophisticated boundaries, some firm, some porous, some malleable, all of critical importance. Our boundaries determine the size and shape and scope of who we are.

When you get sick, that's a boundary violation, and it's pretty easy to tell. A microorganism has passed the physical boundary of your skin, invaded your immune system, and is wreaking havoc where it shouldn't be. Getting well can be thought of as the restoration and strengthening of those boundaries.

Emotional sickness can be harder to recognize and

emotional boundaries can be harder to establish. The trick is to understand how the creation of a boundary needs to be done from a loving place in order to be truly effective. For example, let's say that you're involved with someone who's addicted to drugs or alcohol or gambling or suffering. You've woken up to the fact that you're enabling them; you can see how you support their habit and perversely how your good intentions are negatively impacting their physical health and your emotional well-being. You know you need stronger boundaries, but how do you go about it?

Most people need to get angry, especially at first. This is understandable. Anger is an emotion of self-protection, and in this situation, you need some protection in order to feel safe. However, boundaries sourced in anger are often completely impenetrable. It's almost as if you've discovered an intruder in your house, kicked them out, and then boarded up all of the doors and windows to make sure *that* never happens again.

However, as you can imagine, when you board up your doors and windows you may feel extra safe in the short term, but it's a lot of pain and suffering in the long term. For starters, you can't let anyone in without an incredible amount of effort. This is one of the things we learn in therapy — to feel the hurt and sadness so that we can renovate our emotional home and open our hearts once again. Until we begin this process we are effectively controlled by previous relationships. Letting go of a relationship and establishing new boundaries can be one of the most difficult experiences you'll ever feel your way through, but one of the most rewarding and freeing as well.

Now, we know that the only way to truly let go of something or someone is with love. Yes, you can create a boundary of anger, you can withdraw into an internal cocoon if you need to in order to insulate yourself from your pain. However, anger and withdrawal and denial, while providing sometimes necessary self-protection, do not help you regain your freedom.

Letting go of a person with love means finding understanding and compassion in your heart for them as they truly are — not as you want them to be. With a firm grip on the reality of "what is" you can feel love for them, know that it is time for you to part ways, and let them go. The specific form that takes is up to you. Perhaps you want no contact with them at all. Perhaps you want to limit communication to email or the phone and not see them in person. Perhaps lunch is okay, but certain topics are off limits. Set limits that work for you.

Remember, it's easier to set a firm boundary and relax it than it is to set a flimsy boundary and strengthen it.

However, letting go of the fantasy of the relationship, the fantasy of the future you wish you had, the person you were going to be, the life you were going to lead, the woulda, coulda, shoulda stuff is also important if you want to fully heal from the dissolution of a relationship. Fantasies serve us because they carry information about areas within us that seek our nurturing. In therapy we step outside of our fantasies, examine them, find useful information in them, and then return to our lives to appreciate what is.

Boundaries are tricky whether it's about a romantic relationship, a platonic relationship, or the self-relationship. For example, when the results of my ultrasound came back, Dr. Rosenbloom told me that he could remove half of my testicle, with a small risk of recurrence of the cancer, or he could remove the whole thing and I could get a prosthetic testicle. He said it in a way that implied he was fine with either option, whereas I had a very clear opinion. Take it out! Take it all out! There was no way I was keeping anything questionable in my body.

While that was my first response and what I believe was the correct one for my health, it took some time for me to really deal with the emotional reality of that. I think it may be similar to what a woman goes through who's had a mastectomy. Yes, she can have an implant, and it looks normal, but… but it's not normal and it feels abnormal and it takes some getting used to. I had to let go of a fantasy I didn't even know I had — the fantasy of having a whole and perfect body my whole life. I had to realize that I'm not my testicle, I'm not my body, I'm not even my thoughts. I'm a spiritual being, and I can let go of anything, with love, that threatens my health and spirit. In this case, I thanked my testicle for keeping all of the cancer inside and not letting it spread. I appreciated it for the role it was playing in making me a physically and emotionally healthier person, and I let it go.

I already had strong boundaries regarding diet and drugs and alcohol, and cancer resulted in stronger emotional boundaries regarding relationships with myself and others. Punishing thoughts, difficult clients, poisonous relationships — I became alert to all sorts of toxicity in my life and continued to establish useful boundaries. I reserve the space close to my heart for loving thoughts, delightful clients, connection with God, and healthy intimate relationships with friends, family, and my partner.

What I've learned is that every time I create an artificial boundary, every time I close a door or build a wall, I need to see and appreciate and try to love whatever or whoever is on the other side. I ask myself, "What would love do here?" This reflects reality because, after all, nothing and no one is all bad. Seeing the good means acknowledging the truth of what is, and as soon as that happens appropriate boundaries arise naturally.

chapter 37
GIVING or GETTING?

What happens when your fantasies come true? Ask the big Lotto winners — many of them end up bankrupt or worse off than they were before the big win. Or you could just watch some episodes of *E! True Hollywood Story*. Getting what you think you want — fame, money, success — tends to intensify and magnify your problems, not alleviate them. Look, there's nothing wrong with having fantasies, there's nothing wrong with having problems. But make no mistake, success often creates more pressure to succeed even more, and sooner or later the issues that gave rise to the fantasy in the first place reveal themselves like skeletons crawling out of the closet.

Truly wealthy people, even if they have great financial resources, don't need to give expensive gifts to express their feelings. They give and receive from the heart. True actors can do community theater in Sedona and feel fulfilled. For them, it's not about what they're getting, it's about expressing themselves through their craft, enjoying their personal journey, giving of their creativity, using their experience to allow us to see ourselves in the characters they are portraying. True artists enjoy rehearsal. True athletes enjoy practice. True students enjoy studying. Your pursuit is authentic when your passion is for the process, not the result.

For some of us, the fantasy is fame or fortune or both. For many of us, the fantasy is the perfect marriage, two perfect kids, and a five-bedroom house in a fabulous neighborhood with a white picket fence. It's holidays where our families come together, no one fights, and everyone gets the presents they wanted. But the truth is, even if we achieve the fantasy, it doesn't make us whole the way we'd hoped. Peace doesn't come through external attainment. Internal harmony, self-love, acceptance, being comfortable in our own skin, gratitude for being alive — no one can give these to us. It must come from within; we must give to ourselves.

You see, a fantasy is a response to suffering. It's a mirage of what would heal our wounds, fill our voids, soothe, numb, make the pain go away. A fantasy makes us feel better temporarily; it gives us a false sense of power and importance, like we could right a wrong that's been done to us. We start fantasizing when we're kids. It's natural. But as time goes on the fantasies become larger, more fleshed out with details, more important, and more easily mistaken for our dreams — and dreams, my friends, are entirely different from fantasies.

A dream is sourced in the acknowledgment and appreciation of who you are. A fantasy is about becoming someone or something you're not. A dream is an authentic way of living in the present. A fantasy is the illusory future life that is perfect and without obstacles. A dream is enough even when it's only for you. A fantasy requires that you prove yourself to others. A fantasy is a plan of your own design to heal the deep wounds inside. A dream is a plan of God's design that actually does heal. A fantasy involves leaving the pain behind. A dream involves learning from the pain, using the pain, appreciating it, embracing it because the pain is part of you and because you deserve to be free. The fun of a fantasy is in the outcome. The fun of a dream is in the process. A fantasy involves getting a result for yourself. A dream involves giving to yourself and others.

What do you want out of this life? Is it a vision of getting, or giving?

chapter 38
SOMEWHERE over the RAINBOW

God lives within you. Our relationship with God is our relationship with ourselves, and each relationship is unique because each of us is unique. Faith is, therefore, intensely personal. How you relate to God or the Universal Creative Force or to the big bearded guy that lives in the sky is truly up to you, and that relationship is the foundation of your authentic self and the chief variable that determines the quality of your life. Faith is a big deal.

Here's a way to think about this: when you were born, your world revolved around mom (your primary caregiver). Mom fed you and cared for you and changed your diapers and saw to all your needs. She taught you not to touch the hot stove and to look both ways before crossing the street and how many cookies you could eat after dinner and which vase she'd be really pissed if you broke — mom determined your entire world.

Then, one day, you go to school, and for many years after, your world revolves around culture. You copy the behaviors of your friends. You see what other people's homes look like. You obey new rules in school and in after-school programs and activities. You are rewarded for some things and punished for others. You absorb an incredible amount of factual information about the world, but we know what you really learn. You learn that it's important to be… Rich. Thin. Attractive. Smart. Cool. Healthy. Tall. Sexy. Popular. You learn never to admit you need help. Instead, you learn how to use make-up to hide zits, which clothes are "in" and which are "so last season," which restaurants are "hot," what jobs are "not." You learn to weigh and measure yourself and everyone else in your world.

Most of us get trapped here. We never progress, in terms of wisdom, beyond our early years. Sure, we make more money and have more responsibilities, our relationships get longer and more "serious," maybe we even have children. But that doesn't mean we have wisdom or faith or that we are truly adults. We think that we're making choices in the moment but really we're rehashing old decisions over and over again. We follow the same relationship patterns, we preserve the same family dramas, we recreate old traumas in new ways, we manifest and re-manifest situations sourced in wounds and misinformation acquired in the past. Unresolved pain and suffering structures our lives. Real choice hasn't even entered the picture yet. We're on unconscious auto-pilot.

But for some of us, there comes a time when the structure provided by the past is no longer sufficient. This often occurs in a moment of extreme pain, perhaps a relationship catastrophe or a health crisis, perhaps simply a long dark night of the soul. Then, for just a moment, the light goes on and we wake up and say, "Okay. I've had enough. This is my world and I get to make choices. Now — who am I and what do I want?"

This is the beginning of a wonderful journey, one of relationship with ourselves and relationship with divinity, and yet it is not an easy one. For starters, when we ask ourselves who we truly are, many of us are really asking ourselves, how do I begin to love me? It takes time to admit that we don't know who we are and still to know that we deserve our own love and support and compassion regardless. When we ask ourselves what we want, many of us are really asking, what is my fantasy of wholeness and how can I go about getting there? It takes time to admit that we don't really want a non-existent fantasy, but a sometimes painful, often wonderful reality, a reality of giving to ourselves and others and enjoying the process.

Faith doesn't mean you feel good. It's not peace or grace. Faith is knowing that everything is already taken care of and as it should be. It is an openness to the moment — very similar to the definition of authenticity, which is being your true self in each moment, whoever you are and however you feel at that time. Having faith is inextricable from being an authentic person.

We must learn to appreciate crisis. Often a crisis is what is required to get us to learn how to stop the ceaseless doing and simply surrender into BEING. We all have at least one crisis in our lives, many of us more than one, and the value of the crisis is that sometimes we cannot let go until we have suffered so intensely that letting go is the only remaining option — and then we experience the grace of God.

Let me ask you something. You've been through some hard times in your life, right? Are you still here, reading these words? Haven't you always made it through? Yes, you may be bitter about the pain you've experienced or continue to experience. You may be resentful. I know just how that feels.

I remember when I really started to take my eating disorder seriously. Was it fun? No. Was I bitter? You bet. I'd been devoted to the philosophy of AA for seven years and was completely sober. I had already worked with various psychologists and coaches. I went to Life-Spring. I listened to Tony Robbins. I dieted a la Jenny Craig. I should have been spiritually in balance and healed by then — at least, that's what I thought.

But I was still putting my fingers down my throat to feel better. I was desperate and frustrated to the point of hopelessness. But eventually, I did what we all must do. I dropped to my knees. I admitted that this was larger than me, that I couldn't control it, I couldn't fix it, I couldn't do it on my own. And then something larger than me allowed me to let go. Then I called the Radar Institute and began outpatient therapy with a counselor they recommended.

My point is this: everything that happens is happening *for* you, not *to* you. You are surrounded by great opportunity to have what you really want. Not only the goals in your future, but the acceptance of what is. Faith. Inner balance. A relationship with yourself, with

God. The world, even if it's seemingly against you, even if you can't seem to achieve your goals or fulfill your responsibilities, even if you feel humiliated and stupid and crazy and alone, is *for* you. Trust.

One of the ways I deepen my faith is to really feel my feelings. Like you, I feel hurt and disappointed sometimes. Sometimes I feel rage or grief. Sometimes I'm filled with complicated emotions I don't even know how to label, like intermingling flavors I can't identify. But I know that whatever is happening is happening for a reason, and I remember that as awful as anything has been, I've always made it through. I trust in God so I don't try to avoid my feelings; I do my best to feel them.

Another way I deepen my faith is to listen to my inner guidance. When I am having a hard time with something I ask God for the lesson, and then I listen. Sometimes the courier will be one of my clients, a picture from the collage on my bulletin board, a song on the radio, and then suddenly, aha! My inner guidance speaks. Perhaps you think that's a little silly, but I believe that while God's methods are mysterious, he communicates to us in ways we can understand. "Coincidences" can be divine.

I don't know what to do, sometimes, about the conditions in the world, about the horrible things people do to each other in war or in prison or on playgrounds. I don't know what to do sometimes about the self-inflicted suffering that takes place inside my own mind. Then I take a moment to breathe. I remember that the world is bigger than I am. I remember to trust, to have faith. I feel my feelings. I stop trying to do more, to fix myself or others, and I allow myself to just be.

This is why I am writing this book. In a dark moment I received guidance that sharing what I've learned is the next step on my journey, and my faith allows me to go where I am led. Will there be peace on Earth? Will we stop killing each other? Will I be happy tomorrow? I don't know, but in this moment, I enjoy writing these words. I enjoy sharing myself with you. I enjoy making an effort to be of service to you in your life. And yet, I know that I can't give you my faith. All I can do is share from my experience and pray that you find your own way.

chapter 39
The CONTRIBUTION
No One Else CAN MAKE

Pain is not an enemy. Pain is a teacher. Pain, loneliness, hopelessness, confusion, and all kinds of suffering are the attempts of the Universe to help you feel all of your feelings, to strengthen your faith, to have peace within the deepest levels of yourself so that you can live your life in freedom. Pain gives you permission to BE.

In our culture, we often think of freedom as the right to say or do whatever we want, provided we don't hurt others. But that kind of freedom is potential. True freedom implies action. Freedom isn't just about having options, it's trusting yourself to select from those options as you like without defining yourself on the basis of your results. Freedom requires risk. Freedom implies failing. After all, what kind of success isn't built on failure? What kind of love or intimacy doesn't require risk?

I believe that we're all whole, perfect, and beautiful exactly as we are. This is our birthright and it's just waiting to be claimed. I also believe that 98 percent of our lives is working and that 2 percent may need some adjustments, but I find that many people who walk this earth never truly focus on the 98 percent that's magnificent and working and then manifest more of that for themselves. Instead, they take that 2 percent, focus on it, and make that the 100 percent that they live from, thereby manifesting more of that for themselves. What would it be like to graduate from the School of Struggle and Suffering? To already have your degree? What is your life going to be like when you begin to focus on the 98 percent that's amazing? What's possible now?

The contribution no one else can make is your life, lived this moment, in freedom. This is not an insignificant thing. We sometimes think of contributions like results, as if what you contribute to life is like what you contribute to public television or the Red Cross. The real contribution you make is being an example. When you have the courage to shine your own light, you help others to do the same. Take care of yourself and, in doing so, take care of the world.

What does it mean to be an example? It means that you do the best you can with what you've got, wherever you are. Perhaps you're overwhelmed. Accept it. That doesn't mean tolerate it or pretend that it doesn't bother you. Acceptance isn't a bowl of cherries. Accepting "what is" means feeling the overwhelming feelings and perhaps the pain, despair, and emptiness that accompany them; appreciating all emotions as teachers, still taking care of your professional considerations, still fulfilling your personal commitments, still loving yourself and taking care of yourself to the best of your ability.

The hardest part of being an example is to actually feel our feelings. Sometimes we fool ourselves. We try to feel, but we only end up reporting our feelings. It's easy to tell the difference. If you can describe your feelings, but you don't experience a change of state, you're reporting. Ever watch the *Price Is Right?* Some people win and you see how elated they are. Some win and they don't seem to care. But they do care; it's just that when it's hard to feel pain, it's also hard to feel pleasure. It's hard to feel at all.

You know you're feeling your feelings, not reporting on them, when you experience many different feelings during the course of a day. If you're sharing feelings with a friend, they will be completely engaged and connected. If you're feeling your feelings, you aren't judging them or evaluating yourself. You're just present in the moment, feeling. If there's *one* thing you take away from this book, please remember the importance of feeling your feelings, not simply reporting.

When we're not able to feel feelings, we distract ourselves. I think of distractions as training grounds for consciousness — addictions to food, drugs, shopping, drama, alcohol, emergencies, work, sex, or whatever else. I've definitely done my drugs, drank my liquor, wrecked my cars, and done my time. I'm not proud of it, but I'm not ashamed of it either. I couldn't be the man that I am today had I not had each and every experience that led me to where I'm at now in my life. I am grateful for my past and the lessons that each experience carried for me.

Addictions work in the short term and provide painful lessons in the long term. There isn't enough money in the world to make the deep pain go away; we all know rich, powerful people who are an inch away from throwing themselves off a bridge. You can't be thin enough or famous enough either. Just take a stroll through a Hollywood rehab clinic. There's no amount of sex, no magical pill, no amount of binge food. Believe me. If distractions worked you'd see news headlines like, "Wife drinks her way through painful divorce into great new relationship." Hey, how many gallons of ice cream does it take to make yourself feel better? Zero, it turns out. But do what you have to do. Your distractions aren't things you must get rid of. They are to be appreciated and learned from in order to be free.

Join me in creating limitless opportunities for yourself. The contribution no one else can make is your life, lived in freedom. Who knows what that might look like? Who knows how much fun you will have along the way? Who knows how many other people you will inspire? Who knows how much love you will give and receive?

I'm finding out for myself. I invite you to do the same.

ACKNOWLEDGMENTS

For my clients, I am forever grateful. I feel privileged that you have endowed me with such trust and that you have allowed me the gift of your vulnerability. Thank you for making our relationship a two-way street. I honor you, respect you, and I offer you my complete gratitude. I couldn't be the man that I am today if it weren't for each and every one of you and the experiences that we shared.

Rhett, you are light in my heart and nourishment in my soul. I cherish our love, faith, trust, and understanding. The opportunity to share my journey with you makes me the luckiest man on this planet.

Mom and Dave, you are my number-one fans. Thank you for your unconditional love and support. I cannot imagine my life without you in it.

Dwayne, you are one of the most generous human beings that I have ever had the privilege of knowing. Your friendship means the world to me.

Granny Goose, you are my shining star.

Alan Baker and Beth Kuchar of Rapture Studio, you are the cavalry. Your honor and integrity are impeccable.

My family and friends, you are all amazing, and I love you with all of my heart.

Kitty, I relish the laughter and color that you bring to my world.

Floyd's Barbershop, your generosity of Spirit is inspiring.

Annie, thank you for just being you.

And to Ben Taxy, you are my homerun hitter. Your genius and talent are immeasurable. Thank you for all that you continue to teach me.

ABOUT the AUTHOR

Michael Blomsterberg has been a professional hairapist for 22 years and has received "Certified Life Coach" designation from Coach For Life, an International Coaching Federation (ICF) approved program. As a child he survived physical and psychological abuse. As an adolescent he survived bulimarexia, drug and alcohol addiction, and bankruptcy. As an adult he survived testicular cancer and the dissolution of a 12-year relationship.

His mission is the synergy of his life experience and professional training: to harness his understandings to contribute to the lives of others. He lives with his partner, Rhett, in Southern California.

Ordering Information

MLR Publishing books are available online
and at your favorite bookstore. Quantity discounts are
available to qualifying institutions. MLR Publishing
books are available to the booktrade and educators
through all major wholesalers.

For more information, contact MLR Publishing at
8033 Sunset Blvd. #817, Los Angeles, CA 90046-2401
Call 323-876-3334, or visit

www.hairapy.com *or* www.hairapybook.com

HAIRAPY

DEEPER THAN THE ROOTS

Book Summary

Buy the Book

Excerpts

About the Author

Contact

Do you try to fill your emptiness with endless
activity, retail therapy, and mild (or even serious)
addictions?

Do you feel limited by the traumatic experiences of
your past?

Hairapy: Deeper than the Roots is a book that empowers
you to change your life. Michael Blomsterberg has
consolidated over two decades of hairapy experience into
compassionate, enjoyable essays full of provocative
questions and humorous perspective. This wise and
insightful book will fill the toolbox in your mind with useful
ideas, connect you at a heart-level to your authentic self,
and create limitless possibilities for who you know yourself
to be.

Take a little of the magic of the salon with you wherever you go—and inspire others through your
own courageous example.

*Hairapy: Deeper than the Roots is
available in bookstores now!*

Copyright @2005 Hairapy. All rights reserved. Website designed by Rapture Studio.